PDA IN THE FAMILY

of related interest

The Family Experience of PDA
An Illustrated Guide to Pathological Demand Avoidance
Eliza Fricker
Foreword by Ruth Fidler
ISBN 978 1 78775 677 9
eISBN 978 1 78775 678 6

Can't Not Won't
A Story About A Child Who Couldn't Go To School
Eliza Fricker
ISBN 978 1 83997 520 2
eISBN 978 1 83997 521 9

Being Julia
A Personal Account of Living with Pathological Demand Avoidance
Ruth Fidler and Julia Daunt
Foreword by Dr Judy Eaton
ISBN 978 1 84905 681 6
eISBN 978 1 78450 188 4

The Panda on PDA
A Children's Introduction to Pathological Demand Avoidance
Glòria Durà-Vilà
Illustrated by Rebecca Tatternorth
ISBN 978 1 83997 006 1
eISBN 978 1 83997 007 8

First published in Great Britain in 2024 by Jessica Kingsley Publishers
An imprint of John Murray Press

1

Copyright © Steph Curtis 2024

Foreword Copyright © Julia Daunt 2024

Key features of PDA list on pp.39–40 © PDA Society. This list is reproduced with
kind permission from the PDA Society. This information is published in full at www.
pdasociety.org.uk

Content Warning: This book mentions anxiety and depression.

A CIP catalogue record for this title is available from the British Library and the
Library of Congress

ISBN 978 1 83997 189 1
eISBN 978 1 83997 190 7

Printed and bound in Great Britain by TJ Books Limited

Jessica Kingsley Publishers
Carmelite House
50 Victoria Embankment
London EC4Y 0DZ

www.jkp.com

John Murray Press
Part of Hodder & Stoughton Ltd
An Hachette Company

PDA IN THE FAMILY

FAMILY

Life After the Lightbulb Moment

STEPH CURTIS

FOREWORD BY JULIA DAUNT

Jessica Kingsley Publishers
London and Philadelphia

CONTENTS

Foreword by Julia Daunt   7
Acknowledgements   9
Introduction   13

Ch 1: An Autism Diagnosis   21
Ch 2: Pathological Demand Avoidance   35
Ch 3: The Early Years: Birth to Age Five   57
Ch 4: The Mainstream School Years: Age Five to Ten   83
Ch 5: Not Fine in School   103
Ch 6: Anxiety and Mental Health   127
Ch 7: Sensory Issues   153
Ch 8: Siblings, Family and Friend Relationships   171
Ch 9: Life as a Dud: A Father's Perspective   189
Ch 10: Dealing with Other People   203
Ch 11: What Works for Us   215

Epilogue: The Future   233

FOREWORD

I first met Steph in person at the National Autistic Society PDA conference in 2013 but we had been speaking online via Facebook for a few years before this. I've keenly followed her family by way of her blog, and I've learnt so much from her. I'm proud to call her my friend.

I was very humbled when Steph asked me to write the foreword to this book and I jumped at the chance. Personal insights like this are invaluable and, as a PDAer myself, I'm always interested to read and hear about others' experiences, particularly within a family unit.

PDA in the Family is an inspirational book filled with great stories of family life with a PDAer. It's extremely well written, flows beautifully and is packed with helpful tips and approaches that are clear and easy to apply to your own family life. I had so many 'aha!' and 'ditto!' moments reading it and could directly relate to so much, especially the school stories.

I believe that this book is a must-read for anyone with a connection to PDA: parents, carers and those working with families. It will have you nodding, crying, laughing and raising a glass to Sasha's delightful independence!

Julia Daunt, author of *Being Julia: A Personal Account of Living with Pathological Demand Avoidance*

ACKNOWLEDGEMENTS

To my two girls, Tamsin and Sasha, I love you both the most. I am so proud of how you are making your way through life, and coping with the challenges that society throws at you. You are both amazingly creative, strong and witty – I think you have inherited at least two of those qualities from your Dad and me, but we may have to look further afield for the source of your artistic skills! You have both taught me much about life and this world we live in. Being your Mum is the best job ever and a great privilege.

To the best Mum and Dad in the world, ever, thank you for giving me the best start in life and for showering me with love. You gave me a solid foundation and the strength to find the way forward. Thank you for all you have done for us as a family along the way, from babysitting and childminding to stripping wallpaper and being there for us on holidays. I will be forever grateful for your unwavering support and confidence in my ability to parent my children in the way that they needed. I am so lucky to have had you and I love you so much.

To my husband Chris, thank you for taking the time to write the best chapter of this book. I always knew your writing would be better than mine! Men don't seem to share their feelings very often, so I think what you have written will be appreciated more widely because it could help other partners to feel less alone. Thank you for being a great Dad to the girls; for providing for us by working hard and not minding (much) that me having to stay home with the girls meant I wasn't able to match you in terms of monetary income to our household. More than that, thank you for backing me up when necessary, for adopting a different mindset and not insisting on 'typical' parenting, and for believing that I was doing the best for both our girls.

To my brothers and their partners, family-in-law and other family members, thank you for listening and understanding the varied struggles we face on a daily basis, and for not judging us when we have had to do things differently with our girls. Despite the fact we haven't been able to spend as much time with you as we would have liked to, your ongoing love and support has been apparent and very much appreciated.

To my closest friends, old and new, thank you for not thinking I was crazy. Thank you for keeping me going by allowing me to share the bad times and the good, and for being great sounding boards and voices of reason whilst always being on my side. Love you all!

To Julia, thank you for taking the time to read this book and for writing such a fabulous foreword. I appreciate the effort that must have taken and I am grateful for your thoughts. It was a pleasure to meet you all those years ago and we are thankful that you chose to share your experiences of PDA so that we could understand our daughter better.

To all the members of staff at the schools Sasha has attended who have treated her with compassion, patience and love, thank you. Your understanding helped us move forward as a family at times when we needed support the most. For one teaching assistant in particular, Mrs Storey, thank you for the patience you showed in listening and learning from Sasha, and for communicating so well with us as a family. You helped Sasha develop and progress, and in doing so made a real difference to all of us.

ACKNOWLEDGEMENTS

To all the team at the PDA Society, thank you on behalf of so many other families like mine who have been able to turn to you for information and advice when times are tough. You provide assistance in the best way possible, always with compassion and a true understanding of what families like ours are facing. Sharing information and changing the minds of others has such a big effect on the lives of our PDA children. Please keep up the great work!

Writing a book was much harder than I expected – very different to creating shorter blog posts and sharing thoughts on my social media pages. Thank you to all the team at Jessica Kingsley Publishers who have helped me – extra special thanks to my Publishing Director Lisa Clark for your patience and all your helpful suggestions during the whole process.

Last but not least, to all the people I have had the good fortune to come across online, ever since I first started blogging about our family life – other bloggers, families in similar situations, and generally lovely people who have been open to learning more about PDA. You have all helped to make a huge difference to our lives and to many others. I have appreciated every like, comment and share of my blog and social media pages. Thank you for all the support and for the many lovely messages I have received over the years. Without you, this book would never have been written.

INTRODUCTION

Hi, I'm Steph and I have two girls. My eldest daughter, Tamsin, is 17 years old and my youngest daughter, Sasha, is 15 years old. This is how I introduce myself these days, at events where I am being asked to share my experiences as a parent. I am 50 years old, with silver-grey hair and a fair amount of life experience before I gave birth to my daughters in my early thirties, but my memories of life before having children tend to fade into the background now. I was born and brought up in the North of England where my two brothers and I enjoyed a happy family life with my parents, then I went off to study at Aston University in Birmingham. After finishing my degree, I met and married Chris (who hails from the South of England), and after a short spell living and working in first the Midlands and then the North, we ended up living close to London. This is where we started our family, and this is where I sometimes feel like the odd one out, living in a house where everyone else has a much better memory than me, and where they all pronounce bath as 'barth' and glass as 'glarss'.

Before having children, I wasn't sure that I would know how to be a good mum. My own mum had been a wonderful, loving parent though, and I knew her support would help me figure it out somehow. I had no reason to think that the types of parenting approaches that my parents had used for me and my brothers wouldn't work for my children too. However, my eyes were about to be opened, in a way I had not expected.

Our first child, Tamsin, was a gorgeous, cuddly baby who liked to sleep a lot initially. The pregnancy had been fairly straightforward with only a short period of morning sickness and then Tamsin arrived, exactly on her due date, with a full head of hair. As she grew, Tamsin appeared to be a quick learner who was quiet and eager to please. She loved life and made us smile a lot; she was an easy introduction to parenting for me. I began to ease into the role of mum, believing that maybe I had been made for this after all. Tamsin achieved all her milestones of walking and talking at the suggested ages and she loved us to read bedtime stories for an hour or more – anything to extend that bedtime routine and be with us. Daytimes were full of fun and chatter and typical baby and toddler activities. We would often receive compliments on what a lovely child Tamsin was. Life was full of learning and was always busy in that way it is for every first-time parent, but nothing felt too challenging.

Two years later our second daughter, Sasha, was born. Also on her due date, after another uncomplicated pregnancy, but the labour time with Sasha was much shorter than it had been with Tamsin. I have reflected since that each labour was fitting in its own way – long and steady for our cautious first-born, but much quicker for our determined, impatient second girl who decided exactly when she was ready to be born, with no hanging around. Sasha had masses of soft dark hair on her head too, just like her sister. After an initial cry she settled fairly quickly, although she appeared not to need sleep in the same way our eldest had. We assumed we would know what to do with another little girl, but as you will see, we were soon to find ourselves on a steep learning curve.

The word autism was first mentioned to me when Sasha was two years and seven months old. We had an appointment with a paediatrician who attempted some basic testing of Sasha's skills. The results showed that Sasha did not respond in the way many other children of that age would have done. As the paediatrician discussed her observations that day with me, she mentioned the areas of concern. Significant language delay, highly self-directed behaviours, difficulties with transition and poor social interaction. She suggested that our daughter might be diagnosed as autistic.

Before going to see the paediatrician, I knew very little about autism. I didn't know of anyone else who was autistic. I suspect, like many people of my age, the only reason I knew anything at all about autism was because of the film *Rain Man*. I had watched Dustin Hoffman play the part of Raymond, an autistic man who adhered to strict routines and who showed little emotional expression except when in distress. Over the months and years following our daughter's diagnosis I came to understand that the Raymond character only portrayed certain aspects of autism. Our daughter did not share many of his characteristics.

I think I was still in shock when I returned home from the first appointment with the paediatrician. I impulsively decided to start writing about it, and that was the day my blog was born. I named the blog *Steph's Two Girls* partly because it was difficult to find a website name to do with parenting and autism that wasn't already taken by someone else, but also because I instinctively knew that the autism diagnosis for Sasha would have a big impact on her sister's life too. My initial intention was to keep the blog as an online diary, a place to keep a record of answers to all the questions I had already been asked multiple times up to that point. Questions such as: what kind of a pregnancy and birth it had been; did Sasha respond when I called her name; did she point or take me by the hand when she wanted something; what was her eye contact like? I was hoping not to have to repeat all these answers at every future meeting with a professional, but I somehow guessed that would happen regardless.

For that reason, I decided it might be better if I had the answers noted somewhere in case my memory failed me.

After a few weeks I began to feel that the 'standard' definitions of autism, such as those I saw on the National Autistic Society website at the time, did not seem to describe our daughter very well. Some articles we read online suggested that autistic children did not smile or respond to other people's emotions, they could not give eye contact, they were not sociable and that they might have repetitive movements. None of these descriptions of autism applied to Sasha.

What came next for me was numerous late night research sessions on the Internet and these eventually led to me stumbling across an online group (now a charity known as the PDA Society), where parents and carers were discussing how their autistic children behaved in a variety of situations. Comments were being exchanged about how these behaviours could be directly related to the characteristics of Pathological Demand Avoidance (PDA). The descriptions of PDA seemed to fit our daughter like a glove, in ways that the general autism indicators had not. I explore this in more detail in Chapter 2, but it is worth noting here that those three little letters have played a big part in our family's life since that day. Understanding PDA led to a better understanding of our daughter and enabled us to support her in ways we might not have otherwise considered.

Through my blog I wanted to explain how Sasha's behaviour differed from other children of her own age. I realized that unless you were spending a lot of time with our girl, it was difficult to understand what was going on for her. In many ways Sasha's behaviour appeared similar to other toddlers and my reactions to her meltdowns might not have made sense to other parents who probably assumed she was showing typical toddler tantrum behaviours. So I felt a need to justify and give reasons for both Sasha's behaviour and mine. As I suspect is the case for most parents of children with additional needs, I often felt judged, and I assumed that other people were thinking that I wasn't trying hard enough to manage behaviour or teach my own child the basics. I felt relieved that we had an older daughter who was learning and behaving in more typical ways. Up until diagnosis I had felt slightly confused about why the traditional parenting methods I was using for Tamsin simply were not working for Sasha. It didn't make sense, until I learned about autism and PDA and began to understand the different way in which our younger daughter was experiencing life.

Thirteen years later I am still writing that blog and sharing examples of our life on social media. I have often said that the blog was a form of free therapy for me in the early years, a way of sharing my thoughts and feelings. Apart from keeping it as a diary for us, I wanted to educate people about how our younger daughter was experiencing life differently. I wanted to explain to family, friends and those in the wider community why Sasha acted and reacted the way she did, in the hope that understanding her better would help smooth her path through life.

My hope is that this book will provide some advice and support for other families with children who display similar characteristics to Sasha. Some children might not meet the criteria for a PDA diagnosis but could still have some of the characteristics that make up this profile, and other children might be on long waiting lists for assessments, but whatever the situation it is likely that modifying our expectations of how we expect parenting to go can lead to a calmer, happier life. Typical parenting approaches do not help PDA children, and the more we can reduce the expectations we put on our children, the better. Understanding and compassion can make a big difference. Once we know what works best for our child, it becomes easier to stand strong and have the confidence to educate other people around us.

By opening up about our experiences I hope I can help other people understand the impact that Pathological Demand Avoidance can have on everyday life. Some might think I'm being too optimistic when I say that I hope this book will also reach people who work in education or healthcare settings, but that is a big wish of mine. Understanding PDA is key to supporting some individuals, and sometimes even small changes in communication with PDA children and their families can make a big difference. One phrase I have heard said to several parents over the years is 'if we let your child do that, all the other children will want to do it too'. However, accommodating the differing needs of one child does not have to negatively impact other children when it comes to education. We found that other children were very understanding and accepting of our daughter's differences.

I thought long and hard about whether to share our personal experiences, particularly those regarding the education system, but I concluded that it is important to speak up and acknowledge what is happening in order for there to be any chance of change. I have interacted with many great educators and practitioners who are interested in learning about the individual child they work with, but have also sadly met some with a disappointing attitude, who have not taken the time to listen. Society continues to improve for the better on the whole, I feel, but some people seem to lack the patience to learn why children might behave in different ways. Too many parents are blamed too quickly and too harshly. I hope for a future where our daughter and others like her are not unfairly judged for their actions and reactions. I want them to be treated as highly valuable members of society and for their thoughts and feelings to be acknowledged as a very real way of experiencing life.

Hindsight is a wonderful thing; after agreeing to write this book and finishing most of it, I realized that I am not sure whether it is a good idea for Sasha to read it. Given that she is not a fan of books, the chances of her doing so are quite slim! I have however written it in the knowledge that she may one day choose to pick it up. She has read and enjoyed many of my blog posts, particularly those that remind her of different experiences we have had. We have spoken about how this book is not a simple story of our life but a description of different situations we have faced along the way since her birth, looking through the lens I have as a parent of a PDA child. As much as I would have liked to write about everything from only a positive angle, that would not have been valuable in terms of helping others to understand about the challenges Sasha faces and why she might react differently to other individuals in certain situations. I would love for her to be able to write a book about her experiences from her viewpoint but I think it more likely that she will express herself in different ways. One example of this is an animation she has already produced and published on YouTube, sharing thoughts about her school experiences.

Sasha has found being at school increasingly difficult over the past few years. The reasons for this are explained in Chapters 4 and 5. She currently spends pretty much all of her time at home because leaving the house to do even simple activities outside is challenging for her. She creates amazing digital art and videos (animation is her favourite format) and she sets her own targets to complete a variety of projects. We know that she also likes to write (type) fiction, although we are still waiting to be allowed to read that. She is very talented and her skills are largely self-taught. She is witty, determined, resourceful, intelligent, imaginative, creative, charming and caring. I would use all those same adjectives about our older daughter too, so maybe I am just a little bit biased! But I think others would agree with me regarding both.

So now let me take you back to when Sasha was a baby, and tell you about how we found ourselves visiting a paediatrician for the first time...

Chapter 1
AN AUTISM DIAGNoSIS

During the first 12 months of her life Sasha appeared to be more independent than her older sister in certain respects. She was affectionate and loving but seemed happier with her own company than Tamsin had been. Some days she was passive, content to stay where she was, not requesting anything, but other days she was curious, with no apparent worries about exploring outside her immediate area. Our two girls played and interacted well with each other and we have plenty of photos and videos of them laughing and having fun together at this age. Occasionally Sasha would become upset and we struggled to work out why, but we were not concerned with her behaviour in any way. We simply assumed that our girls had distinctive and different personalities, as most siblings do. I have often wondered if people might think that the autistic traits must have been very obvious for Sasha to be diagnosed at such a young age, but to us and other family and friends around us, she appeared to be growing up like any other typical toddler.

The only indication that development was progressing more slowly for Sasha was her language ability. Although she was vocal, she used a lot of babble and jargon and had very few, if any, clear words. This was unlike our experience with our older daughter, whose speech had been clear and well-constructed from an earlier age. At times it felt as though Sasha had developed her own language. She made plenty of sounds and tried to communicate with us, but lots of her words were unrecognizable and it could be difficult to understand her.

In those days, it was standard procedure for children to have a health check around the age of two years old. We mentioned our concerns about speech and hearing to the lovely health visitor who came to our house to check Sasha over, but her response was simply that 'all children develop at different rates and in their own time'. Which is of course true, but didn't help us much at that point. We were told that we would need to wait another six months before our daughter would be referred for speech therapy by the health visitor team.

Sasha was only using around 20 spoken words by this stage and many of those weren't clear to people outside of the home. 'Bubble' was one of the three clear words she did have, along with 'mama' and 'dada'. She would say 'ket' for blanket, 'wa' for water, and a hard 'a' along with a pat on the head for hat. Over the following year we realized that Sasha struggled most with the letters 'S' and 'T', which seemed a shame because her sister was called Tamsin and her favourite toy was Terry! For many months Sasha would use a completely different word for her sister's name, something which sounded like 'Gah-oo', and although we all came to understand who she meant when she said this, we never did find out why she settled on that as her way of saying Tamsin's name.

We felt that the speech delay needed more investigation sooner rather than later. After a quick check online, we discovered that we could self-refer Sasha to the NHS speech therapy service and she was given an initial assessment with a speech therapist around four months later. I am glad we went with our gut instinct and didn't wait for the health visitor to refer us at a later stage. That is my first piece of advice to other parents and carers – trust yourself. If you have any concerns about your child's development, ask for help. Make some short notes with examples of what you think might be unusual or different to what you expected your child to be doing, then speak to a doctor, health visitor or staff at any setting they attend. If their answers still leave you with concerns, keep asking more questions.

Speech and language assessment

I can still clearly picture the layout of the room where we had the first appointment with the speech therapist. Near the door there was a low table and chairs set designed for children, and in the far corner of the room was a bigger desk and chair in front of a computer. Sasha was happy to sit at the small table she was pointed towards as we entered the room and she began playing with the puzzles that were laid out on it. I went to sit in the big chair, which was a bit further away, and Sasha seemed unconcerned about not being right next to me. The speech therapist started asking me all the standard questions (which were to be repeated many times over the coming years): how was the pregnancy, and the birth; were any of us on any medication; what words could Sasha say; what sort of behaviours were we seeing?

I answered the questions as best I could. It took around half an hour and then the speech therapist looked directly at me and asked: 'Have you noticed anything unusual about your daughter since you've been in this room?' I had no idea what she was getting at and probably looked a bit bemused, so she answered her own question for me: 'Sasha hasn't moved from that table or made any sound since you've been in here.' I remember that comment threw me a little. As I pointed out to the therapist, Sasha was quite happy sitting at the table, playing with the toys. We hadn't asked her any questions, so why would she feel the need to talk?

It was only later on at home, when I mulled this situation over a bit more, that I realized that if I had been in that appointment with our first-born daughter at that age, Tamsin wouldn't have been content to stay sitting at the little table. She would have been climbing all over my lap after ten minutes, or at least shown some sort of interest in the person asking me questions. She would have listened to my replies to the therapist. Sasha wasn't in the slightest bit bothered about what I was doing or saying, and she wasn't listening to our conversation at all. She was content doing her own thing, in her own little world.

That was a common thought we had about Sasha when she was young; she was mostly calm and content as long as she was doing an activity she wanted to do. Which would, I think, be the case for many children of that age. It was what happened when she was not happy that gave us cause for concern. Sasha's extreme reactions to situations she wasn't happy with were on a completely different scale to our older daughter's emotions and responses. With hindsight we have realized that part of the reason we found these reactions difficult to deal with was because we often didn't see or understand what had caused the upset in the first place. The distress was rarely about not getting a toy or chocolate that she wanted, and only occasionally because she didn't want to do something we asked her to. More than half the time the problem was not obvious and nothing seemed to make sense.

By the time of that initial speech assessment in October, Sasha had made some progress from when we had approached the service four months earlier. She was using more words, including the names of the Teletubbies and even the odd sentence or phrase such as 'there it is'. But we felt very little of it was clear to anyone outside our home. In our meeting, the speech therapist ran through what language was typically used by two-and-a-half-year-olds, and what sounds they would make. Sasha didn't seem to be that far behind age-appropriate expectations, so overall we weren't particularly concerned. Until a couple of weeks later that is, when we received the speech therapist's initial report from the visit she had made to observe Sasha in her nursery placement.

Sasha was attending a day nursery for a few hours a week, the same setting that her older sister attended at the time. Staff at the nursery had commented that Sasha did not follow one keyword instructions and that her understanding appeared very variable. Their reports stated that she was observed to require a lot of visual prompts to follow instructions and would not consistently follow them. They went on to say that Sasha spent a lot of time on her own at nursery. She didn't play with the other children and often appeared to move away from them when they entered an area she was already in or if they got too close to her.

Conversely, we felt Sasha was quite a sociable baby and toddler when she was with us. Our older daughter was shy and hid behind our legs when meeting new people; it took her a long time to warm up. Sasha wasn't like this and seemed more comfortable around other people than Tamsin did. I remember one occasion, for example, when she happily shouted 'hi' to the postman who was delivering to our next-door neighbour's house. He was new to the job and not someone she had seen before, but that didn't seem to faze her. Sasha would talk to anyone if it was her who was initiating the conversation, but seemed less inclined to respond if others approached her and asked her questions.

The speech therapist's report after the nursery observation suggested a severe expressive and receptive language delay with social communication difficulties. I think I probably blocked the word 'severe' from my mind at that stage, or at least chose to ignore it. The report documented that Sasha didn't interact well with the other children at nursery or use many words when she was there. We were informed that Sasha would be referred for a development check with a paediatrician, but at the same time we were reassured that it was simply a routine part of the process and nothing to worry about.

Hearing tests

Around this time, as well as noticing emerging speech difficulties, we also briefly wondered if there might be a problem with Sasha's hearing. She would respond to her own name, but only sometimes. There were many times when it seemed as if she hadn't heard us, even though we were speaking directly to her. In contrast, we often used to say that if we crinkled a chocolate wrapper in the next room, she would definitely hear that! It was almost as if she was choosing not to listen. She appeared to understand single words and short sentences, but if anything approaching complex language was used, Sasha seemed to 'switch off' and it felt like she was ignoring us. We found out later down the line that hearing tests are quite a common early life experience for many autistic children.

We attended a handful of hearing appointments over the space of a few months, and each time we went to the clinic, I wasn't sure that Sasha would comply with any of the requests properly. At home, we wouldn't always get a response if we asked Sasha to do something. Most of the time I felt that the reason for 'non-compliance' was more likely to be because Sasha hadn't understood, rather than because she simply didn't want to follow the instruction or because she couldn't hear. To be honest, I think we had come to the conclusion that there wasn't a hearing issue even before she took the official tests.

The first hearing check appointment did not go well at all. Sasha point-blank refused to play the 'game' of stacking the blocks on poles when she heard a sound. We had to concede defeat and booked back in for more tests a few weeks later. I suspect the first appointment was a bit too scary for her, too much of the unknown. For the appointments that followed, we were shown to a smaller room with no other distractions and Sasha engaged a little more each time. When the results came back, they suggested only a mild case of glue ear. We were informed that glue ear is quite a common childhood condition and that there was nothing major to worry about in terms of our daughter's hearing. That was a relief in one way, but on the other hand it didn't give us any answers as to why Sasha didn't appear to listen consistently.

The initial speech and language assessment had taken place in late September, before the run-up to Christmas. From then we waited three months for an appointment with the paediatrician. I wrote on my blog a few months later about how those three months went by so slowly and felt like a long time. Now, having heard how much longer other families have had to stay on waiting lists, desperate for their concerns to be heard, I know how lucky we actually were. I didn't stop to think too much about why our daughter had been referred to a paediatrician because my mind was already occupied with buying Christmas presents for the girls and preparing the house for visitors. Although I couldn't put my finger on why, I already knew that the festive period would bring extra challenges for Sasha and that there would be a knock-on effect on the whole family. Of course, now that I've learnt more about autism I understand that some of those challenges could have been due to the big changes in both house appearance and routine. Special occasions like Christmas or birthdays can often lead to periods of increased tension during the run-up to the day, and on the day itself. Back then I had no understanding though, only subconscious thoughts that life around this period was about to become more difficult.

Paediatrician appointment

The upcoming appointment with the paediatrician was at the back of our minds and didn't cause us much worry. Sasha seemed so happy, as she always did, and her speech was developing still further. *Dora the Explorer* was a firm favourite among the DVDs that she watched at home and Sasha would sometimes mention Dora's friends. Her speech sounds were still unclear and one example of this was how she named Dora's friends out loud: Boots the Monkey was 'Boo', Isa was pronounced 'Ee-ha' and Tico was 'eeco'. New general phrases such as 'where mama gone?' were evident, and she could now count up to ten, both forwards and backwards. She could tell us all these numbers clearly in Spanish too, thanks to Dora. For some reason known only to Sasha, she would always leave out the Spanish word for six when counting, even though she knew what it was and how to say it. In English, six was the clearest number but was pronounced 'ix' and seven was 'eben'. To an outsider, the sounds she made for other numbers would not have been instantly recognizable, especially if they were said out of the context of counting to ten. We knew she was able to count to ten however, and we were told by a staff member at the nursery that there were plenty of older children who couldn't count to that level. So we assumed it meant Sasha wasn't delayed in terms of learning.

We were not overly concerned about Sasha's behaviour at this stage, although we did know that it was significantly more challenging than our older daughter's had been. Challenging because her reactions were overall more extreme; they were louder and lasted longer. Sasha didn't display any violence or aggression; she just became extremely agitated or distressed. When Sasha had what others would call a 'tantrum', we always felt it was because she was truly, deeply upset. Often though, we struggled to understand what she was upset about. It rarely felt like a typical toddler tantrum with the sole purpose of getting her own way, although that did happen on occasion too. Over time we came to understand that tantrum is not a helpful word and 'meltdown' is a much better term for many of our daughter's reactions. We recognized the difference between tantrum and meltdown even though back then we didn't have the words to describe these emotions. A meltdown for Sasha usually involved dropping to her knees and bending over, curling up into what we called the 'mushroom' position. Sasha would cry and she would be fixed to the spot, unable to move or be moved. If anyone tried to talk to her or coax her out of it, the crying would intensify, becoming louder and more high-pitched.

One of the forms we were given before seeing the paediatrician asked several questions, including 'does she tolerate changes of routine/clothes?'. My answer was 'not well'. The next question was 'does she have any particular fears or dislikes?' and my reply was 'getting dressed!'. Our first meeting with the paediatrician was an early morning appointment, and I had experienced the usual struggles with trying to persuade Sasha to get dressed before we left home. Despite this, and the fact that we were going into a new building for a reason she couldn't have understood, when we arrived at the paediatrician's door Sasha did walk in calmly and seemingly confident in the new surroundings. She had been happy to examine the play kitchen and accompanying toys in the clinic waiting area; I think she probably thought they were the reason I had taken her to this new place. We didn't have to wait very long to be seen, and thankfully it wasn't far to walk to the room where the paediatrician would be assessing Sasha (walking any distance was never a favourite activity for Sasha). To get to the room we had to go up some stairs where the walls had been painted cheerily with some big paint splashes, and these seemed to amuse Sasha. All of this meant her mood was high when we first walked into the room.

After the paediatrician had a very brief introductory chat with me, Sasha was invited to sit at a small table to play some games with her. We discovered later these were part of something called the Griffiths Mental Development Scales. Rather typically for her, Sasha chose not to sit when asked. The paediatrician's report we received later noted that Sasha had 'pushed her away', although this was not in an aggressive manner. Sasha roamed the small room instead, choosing to return to the table only when something caught her attention. We hadn't been prepared in any way for what might happen during this appointment, so I was as much in the dark as Sasha about what was expected of her. Thinking back now it's easy to realize that the whole event must have seemed bewildering to Sasha. But as I sat and watched the interaction between Sasha and the paediatrician, it occurred to me that our older daughter Tamsin would have sat down obediently when asked and she would have listened to the instructions. She would have enjoyed showing she was able to complete these kinds of tests, which involved simple activities such as sorting small wooden puzzles. One box contained blocks of different shapes and sizes and colours. The paediatrician would ask Sasha to pass her the blue block, for example, or she would start building a tower with blocks decreasing in size and ask Sasha to place the next one. Sasha refused to build a tower for the paediatrician initially, but did build one later on in the session. She refused to play with beads or count the bricks and then became cross when the brick boxes were taken away from her, and she wouldn't do any drawing when asked to, even though she loved drawing at home.

Occasionally, Sasha's interest would be piqued and she would engage with the paediatrician, but only if there was an opportunity to sort by colour or line things up. Very quickly, Sasha seemed to become tired of the attempts at interaction, and she then started to become agitated. She used language which consisted of a lot of jargon and the word 'no' repeated. We always laugh about 'no', because we say it was Sasha's favourite word, but only if she was the one saying it. To this day, she still doesn't like it if we use the word 'no'. Instead, we've had to find a lot of different ways to say 'no' without actually using the word itself, by using phrases such as 'maybe later' or 'I'm not sure if that's possible just now but we'll see if we can do it tomorrow'.

After 15 minutes of the paediatrician attempting to encourage her to complete the tasks, Sasha had had enough. She handed me her coat and took my hand to try to drag me to the door. It was a clear sign she wanted to leave. When she realized we couldn't leave immediately because I needed to stay and talk with the paediatrician, Sasha began to get more distressed. Eventually she clambered up onto a hospital style bed which was in the room and lay there facing the wall, with her coat pulled on top of her.

At that point, all of Sasha's behaviour over the previous two years seemed to swim into focus for me. I realized that I had often been making excuses for her. In situations like this where she refused to join in or follow instructions, I'd say that she was tired. More often than not, we would leave activities at the point when Sasha asked to leave or tried to drag me away. I'd do that because I'd had experience of what happened if I tried to stay – Sasha would become louder and louder with her requests to leave, eventually reaching the point where she would be screeching. Or sometimes she would do what we affectionately called her 'falling asleep trick', in order to avoid engaging. On this occasion though, it was early morning, and it was very clear that it wasn't tiredness which was prompting her actions. It's easy for me to look back now with hindsight and with the knowledge that I've gained and to realize that her withdrawal or extreme emotional outbursts were signs of the stress of everyday demands being placed upon her.

The next month Sasha and I returned for a follow-up appointment, together with Sasha's dad this time. After speaking to us both, the paediatrician confirmed that she believed a diagnosis of autism was appropriate. Her summary after the initial appointment had included the sentence: 'It is difficult to get an accurate assessment of Sasha's developmental skills due to her difficulties accessing the assessment.' The report then continued: 'Her skills do however appear to be age-appropriate. Clearly her language is significantly delayed and she also presents with highly self-directed behaviours, difficulties with transition and poor social interaction.'

After receiving the official diagnosis, I had to pass this news on to family and friends and people working with Sasha. One person looked at me in a sad way and said, 'Oh, Steph, I'm sorry.' At the time I felt anger; I didn't want their pity, I wanted support for my child. I felt it was a negative reaction to the matter-of-fact news I was delivering. The insinuation was that the autism diagnosis was bad and that the future for my daughter was bleak. I am sure the person who made this comment was not intending to upset or offend and I know from personal experience that it can be easy to say the wrong thing at times. From that day on though, I was determined to ignore and dispel any negative feelings regarding autism. Autism is not the problem; autistic brains do not need fixing, it is attitudes and environments that need to change.

I was not in any way prepared for that initial conversation about autism, but it somehow gave me a feeling of relief. Without realizing it, I had already been using many strategies to try to make life manageable for us all at home. I had questioned my own parenting skills, and wondered why it was that our older daughter (who was four at the time) would follow my instructions, but our younger one did not. As we discussed autism, I realized it could explain some of the behaviours that we had seen from Sasha at home. For months we had been subconsciously accommodating Sasha's unusual behaviour in order to avoid the meltdowns. With this new information about the difficulties she might be experiencing and how they were affecting her everyday life, I began to look back and replay our experiences with a fresh pair of eyes. Sasha had already been using a lot of avoidance strategies but I hadn't recognized them as such because I hadn't understood any of the difficulties she was experiencing. Months later, I was to have what is commonly talked about as a 'lightbulb moment' as I discovered information about Pathological Demand Avoidance. More on that in the next chapter.

ADVICE FOR PARENTS AND CARERS

- Keep a diary.

  - Make a note of everyday activities and your child's reactions to them, along with any other behaviour or communication you think is unusual.

  - Use bullet points rather than long descriptions as these will help when you need to explain to professionals who are short of time.

- Take photographs, voice recordings or videos to record actions and communication.

  - These could help show unusual behaviour or non-typical play situations.

  - Voice recordings can give an indication of the kind of speech and language used. They can also reveal whether excessive anxiety is brought on by constant questioning and can be helpful to share a child's views on a specific topic.

  - Filming meltdowns is definitely not recommended, as it is not good to show children in distress and efforts should be concentrated on calming any situations rather than filming. Having a camera pointed their way could lead to more extreme emotional responses from a child.

- Have a plan for how and where on your phone or computer you will store photos, videos and other documents corresponding to your child and situations like this. Using some kind of labelling system can help make them much easier to find when they are needed.

- Ask for help.

  - Don't be pushed away if you still have concerns about your child's development; keep asking questions and request more than one opinion.

- There are two main tools used for diagnosing autism, the ADOS (Autism Diagnostic Observation Schedule) or the DISCO (Diagnostic Interview for Social and Communication Disorders).

  - If your child does not score highly on an ADOS test but you feel they might be masking, it might be worth asking for a second opinion and requesting a DISCO assessment. The DISCO is known to look at wider aspects of the skills of individuals and the challenges they face.

Chapter 2
PATHOLOGICAL DEMAND AVOIDANCE

A s I left the paediatrician's office after Sasha's initial assessment, I was given a leaflet with details of a support group called Spectrum Girls, for parents of autistic girls. I nervously joined a group of around eight other mums who were meeting up for coffee and a chat once a month. They were a source of comfort in the early days; other parents who I could relate to because, like me, they were living a life somewhat different to those who only had neurotypical children.

As these mums chatted about their experiences with their girls, I began to learn more about autism. What struck me every time we met, though, was that I would think, 'Well, those girls sound a little bit like Sasha, but in many ways nothing like her.' I would come home feeling relieved that others understood some of my challenges, but sometimes these meetings left me feeling more confused. Their girls seemed to me to have a lot in common with each other. They liked routine, tended to have obsessions about objects, were anxious and 'on the edge' of social groups, more comfortable being on their own, were very black and white about facts, liked to follow rules and were scared of getting into trouble, and didn't tend to role play or immerse themselves in fantasy worlds. Most of the girls we were talking about seemed to be able to express themselves better at home than our daughter could, and most of them appeared to be masking, at school or in other situations. By that I mean they were trying hard to fit in, or to fly under the radar. Sasha, however, seemed to act in pretty much the same way for nursery staff and for other people as she did at home. I always used to say that 'what you see is what you get with Sasha'. There was definitely no masking at a young age and her avoidance was the same in any situation. Sasha seemed quite different from these other autistic girls.

One of the autistic characteristics discussed within our group that did not seem to apply to Sasha was the idea that autistic children liked routine, and could manage life better if there was a schedule and they were told what was going to happen next. Sasha seemed to thrive on the novelty factor, and spontaneous activities sometimes felt like a bigger success than having a fixed routine. She was only happy with a plan if she had been the one to choose what it was. An example of this was the time I decided to make Sasha some PECS style boards, when her speech was still developing. PECS stands for picture exchange communication system – a tool that uses visual pictures to enable communication without relying on speech. I created a blank weekly schedule, laminated it and stuck it on the wall. It had days of the week across the top, Monday to Sunday, and the AM/lunch/PM/bedtime column down the side. I took photos of places we would go to and everyday items around us, like Sasha's clothes, the preschool setting, her bed and our car. Then I found symbols online for other everyday activities, such as swimming or a toothbrush, and I printed the images out. I laminated them all, cut around every shape, and added Velcro to both the schedule and the backs of the images. On the blank schedule I would stick relevant images for what I proposed we would do at different times during the week coming up. I hoped this would give Sasha some understanding of what was expected and that it would provide some much-needed structure and routine. Well, it did... for approximately two days. As soon as Sasha realized she could reach the planner herself and remove activities she didn't want to do, that was exactly what she did. No more brushing teeth, for starters! Other images were moved around on a daily basis, to suit herself. When I thought that maybe moving the chart out of Sasha's reach would help set those boundaries, it turned out that she would then do her best to totally ignore the schedule. She would become irate if I tried to carry on with plans of what I wanted her to do.

Another way in which our daughter didn't seem to fit the commonly found descriptions of autism available at that time was that she was very sociable and liked being around others, both children and adults. She was less keen on children who were younger than she was, though. I assumed that was due to them being more unpredictable, noisier, and less likely to give Sasha space or follow her lead. Sasha had a great imagination and would make up interactive role-play scenarios with us and her toys, and with other children. This went well as long as she was in charge of what was happening. It was as if she needed that control, or else she fell to pieces. One of her early reports noted that she was inflexible and unable to respond to ideas from others.

PDD-NOS or atypical autism

The initial suggestion of an autism diagnosis by the paediatrician had come as a relief in some way. It felt like an explanation for the different behaviour we were seeing from Sasha compared to our older daughter. But the mums I was meeting at the Spectrum Girls group were describing their girls in ways that sounded quite different to Sasha. I began to wonder if autism was actually the right diagnosis for our daughter. I needed to understand more, so I turned to the Internet and read as much as I could.

During one of my late-night research sessions I read about Pervasive Development Disorder (PDD), which seemed to be an umbrella term for a few different conditions, including autism. That led me on to articles about PDD-NOS (Pervasive Development Disorder Not Otherwise Specified, which is a bit of a mouthful, hence the acronym). From what I understood, PDD-NOS was a diagnosis given to children who did not meet all of the criteria for autism. This term seemed to be more common in America – in Europe the term atypical autism was used instead – to describe those who had some, but not all, of the characteristics of autism. It was the 'not otherwise specified' part of this PDD-NOS term that caught my attention, because I was feeling like Sasha's character did not quite match the standard descriptions of autism I had read.

I ended up following a trail of information to a group called the PDA Contact Forum (now a charity known as the PDA Society). There I found other parents describing children who sound like Sasha in many ways, and that was where I first read the words Pathological Demand Avoidance (PDA). From then on I absorbed as much information on PDA as I could find. I learnt that Professor Elizabeth Newson, a developmental psychologist and international expert in autism, was the first person to identify PDA back in the 1980s. She had seen a substantial number of children in her clinics who seemed to have some, but not all, of the characteristics of autism. She noted that these children tended to have good imaginations and seemed to be sociable, traits that were not usually associated with other autistic profiles. Pathological Demand Avoidance was the term Professor Newson created for her group of children whose behaviour reflected an extreme avoidance of demands. The dictionary definition of pathological is 'not reasonable or sensible, impossible to control or caused by, or connected with, disease or illness'. Some might say pervasive might have been a better first choice of word for this condition, given that the demand avoidance seems to be constantly present, running through all aspects of life for those who experience it. Some people wish that it had been named Extreme Demand Avoidance and others have suggested that Pervasive or Persistent Demand for Autonomy would have been better as an alternative. However, Pathological Demand Avoidance were the words chosen by Elizabeth Newson, and her first peer reviewed publication on PDA appeared in the *Archives of Disease in Childhood* in 2003, entitled 'Pathological Demand Avoidance Syndrome: a necessary distinction within the pervasive developmental disorders'. In 2010, PDA research led by Francesca Happé began at Kings College London, and more research by other practitioners has been published in the years since. I have of course offered to share our family's experiences with anyone and everyone I can, because I think the more that is understood, the better life can be for children like our daughter.

Characteristics of PDA

The PDA Society describes PDA individuals as having 'a need for control which is often anxiety related'. The original list of characteristics of PDA proposed by Professor Newson has changed slightly over time as understanding grows, but many of the aspects noted remain the same. The PDA Society lists the key features of PDA as:

- Resists and avoids the ordinary demands of life
- Uses social strategies as part of the avoidance
- Appears sociable on the surface, but lacking depth in understanding
- Experiences excessive mood swings and impulsivity
- 'Obsessive' behaviour, often focused on other people

- Appears comfortable in role play and pretend, sometimes to an extreme extent.[1]

Resisting and avoiding ordinary demands described exactly what was happening for us on a daily basis. It was not a case of Sasha picking and choosing only the fun things to do in life; she often refused to do simple, everyday things which we knew she loved to do. That included activities such as swimming or going to the park, outings and events which were not part of our agenda but fun places for her to be. Within the home, if we told her to do something simple such as have a drink or eat her food, that could lead to a meltdown. Brushing teeth is just one example of an everyday, ordinary demand that Sasha has always had difficulty with. We came to realize that a major cause of the avoidance was the lack of control she felt she had over any given situation, but driving that was her extremely high level of anxiety.

One particular attribute shared by all the children in the group Elizabeth Newson first studied was that they used social strategies to avoid demands, rather than outright refusal. This was carried out in a variety of ways; such as by using distraction or excuses, physically incapacitating themselves, withdrawing into fantasy, making lots of meaningless noise, repeating back phrases to the adult making demands, or ultimately by having a panic attack which could involve noise or aggression. Sasha would use one or all of these avoidance techniques at different times, instead of simply saying 'no'. Her favourite responses tended to include 'I can't do that' or 'I don't love it' or 'I'm too tired'. She also used the phrase 'I'm bored' regularly, particularly when she didn't understand something.

Several years ago, I attended a conference about PDA, organized by the National Autistic Society. During the event a video was

---

1   © PDA Society. This information is published in full at www.pdasociety.org.uk accessed July 2023.

played, showing a young child in a clinic avoiding all the questions put to him. He was giving answers that a typically developing child probably would not use, such as 'My legs don't work so I can't' when the clinician asked him to come back closer to her from where he was at the other side of the table. It brought tears to my eyes, as I recognized so many similarities with what our girl used to say and do. She would ignore requests so often that we wondered if her hearing was impaired. She would curl up into a mushroom and pretend to go to sleep rather than do what was asked of her. At school it was noted that Sasha would use a variety of language to avoid doing adult-led tasks, and her choice of phrases included 'Ssshh, I'm busy', 'Well, I'm just making an xxx', 'I might do it tomorrow' or 'I take back my promises'. At times she would change the subject and try to distract the person asking the questions or making demands of her. She would repeat back every word I said, with a grin on her face, or stick her fingers in her ears and say 'lalalala' repeatedly.

PDA individuals are described as being sociable on the surface, but with a lack of sense of identity, and underlying difficulties in social interaction and communication. Sasha would literally talk to anyone and seemed to enjoy being around others when she was younger. I remember her once grabbing a postman by the hand, even though she had never met him before! Sasha was definitely sociable and enjoyed being around other people, but she frequently refused to participate in group activities. This obviously made both school and after-school activities difficult. We tried music sessions, dance classes and drama clubs, but although Sasha seemed interested initially, she was unable to join in for any length of time past the first few minutes. She was always very polite, but didn't always follow rules. We sometimes felt as if she saw herself as a mini-teacher, not obliged to do the same as her peers, but this was more a case of her assuming everyone was equal rather than thinking she was on a level above the other children. Her refusal to join in or complete tasks often appeared to be driven by anxiety; a fear of not being able to do the tasks well, fear of getting it wrong, or a lack of understanding of what was being requested. She rarely said no just to be awkward.

Excessive mood swings would happen regularly at home; Sasha could seem perfectly happy one moment, but the next she was suddenly in a state of meltdown. These were not tantrums that would blow over; the knock-on effects could last for hours or even into the next day. Her meltdowns would involve shouting initially, with a very quick escalation to screaming, along with flailing arms and legs, or else she would curl up on the floor into a mushroom shape. At that point she would become a dead weight, and if we tried to move her by lifting her up she would not put her legs down or walk. Some days nothing would make her happy again once she was even slightly upset. The triggers for her meltdowns and upset behaviours were inconsistent and often inexplicable. One example of this is a time when she had asked for a drink. She came to sit at the table to have it but then became distressed, pushing away the drink that she had requested. She actually did want that drink though, and asked for it again two minutes later, leaving us confused as to why she had become so upset. We began to understand that the lack of control caused Sasha great distress, but we could also see that Sasha didn't realize or understand that she was controlling us. It was never intentional, none of her actions came from a position of knowingly wanting control.

I am not a fan of the word obsessive because of its negative connotations. Sasha's behaviour would not be described as obsessive. She had a keen interest in characters such as Dora, Peppa Pig and My Little Pony in the early days, but I am sure many parents could say the same of their neurotypical children. Sasha possibly watched them on repeat a little more often and stayed interested in them a little longer than other children might have. Characters, brands and games such as Minecraft, Nintendo (Kirby, Mario and Splatoon especially) and Pokémon have all entered her life at different stages along the way and are enjoyed in phases, but I would say these have been passions, never obsessions. The only thing we might have said she seemed obsessive about was the need to be in control. Sometimes it felt as if I was her obsession, as the person who understood her best. Over time this developed to a point where she only wanted me to carry out certain routines for her, such as bedtime, or getting her food, and she would refuse to cooperate or eat if someone else tried to help. Nowadays she is less controlling about this perhaps, but she still clearly prefers me to be the one to do everything for her. That is likely to be because she trusts me; she knows I have learnt how to do things exactly as she needs them to be in order for her to feel comfortable.

Having a vivid imagination and an ability to role-play have always been key parts of Sasha's personality. She spends a large amount of time working on imaginative stories and scenarios, and she has created amazing scripts that she hopes will be the basis for a future television or online series.

Delayed speech was a feature of PDA that was on the original characteristics list noted by Elizabeth Newson, but it has since been acknowledged that not all PDA children will have delayed speech or language. Sasha's speech development was different to that of her peers and she showed signs of unusual speech patterns. At the age of five it was reported that some of her language was quite advanced for her age. It sometimes seemed as if she had learned whole phrases to simply repeat, but she did generally manage to use these phrases appropriately. Her speech sounds were still not clear however, and her understanding seemed variable. It is difficult for me to accurately describe her speech and language abilities and how they have progressed over the years in just a few sentences here. Now she is a teenager she talks a lot less and prefers to mostly communicate via text. Although her speech sounds are vastly improved, I think others might pick up on something unusual about how she talks, but it is difficult to explain what it is that makes it different. Her language use in the fiction she types is at an advanced level; her use of a wide range of vocabulary can impress others. When she was younger I remember being amazed at her ability to always say please and thank you at the right times, more regularly than her peers or our older daughter ever did. She would often get confused with pronouns though and she would reply 'I don't know' for any question she didn't want to answer. Linked to this was her attention and listening skills appearing to fluctuate; at school she could answer to the teacher calling her name for the register, despite being involved in another task at the time, but minutes afterwards she would need to be told several times to join in with what the other children were doing.

The lightbulb moment

The lightbulb moment came when I read about PDA and realized that all of these characteristics applied to our daughter. At our first meeting the paediatrician had suggested that Sasha's behaviour was oppositional. Although oppositional might have been considered a relevant choice of word because Sasha often refused to do something for us or others, I couldn't help but feel that this word did not describe her well. I felt the same way about the word naughty. Our girl was not refusing to do things just for the sake of it or for attention; she was rarely intentionally disobedient. When we began to look more carefully at the behaviour and what was happening before any upset, we could recognize some of the reasons for her refusal or avoidance. Some of the difficulties were around sensory issues, such as environments that were too noisy, too big, too much going on, too many people, etc, but there were plenty of other occasions, on a daily basis, where there seemed to be no rhyme or reason for the ensuing meltdowns.

We did not disagree with the autism diagnosis Sasha was given; the overarching features of autism definitely applied, but we did feel that some of the standard descriptions of autism did not seem to fit our daughter. The typical strategies for helping autistic children brought varying degrees of success. For example, as described earlier, although Sasha liked to see a visual timetable when she was younger, and a 'now and next' board helped to clarify plans for her, she did not like to be told she had to stick to those. She wasn't a fan of consistent, imposed routines; she was happy to swap and change what was happening on a whim, as long as it was *her* whim.

The main challenge for Sasha and for us was control. Sasha had a need to have things exactly as she wanted them, and there did not always appear to be a logical reason for what she wanted. Some of these needs could be explained by general autistic traits, such as liking routine, or sensory issues, but at other times they seemed to be driven purely by the need for control. She *needed* her choice of music in the car and to sit in the front seat, *needed* to have a picnic blanket laid completely flat with no wrinkles at all, and *needed* to win any games we played as a family. We had to allow her that high level of control over many aspects of life because if we did not, the meltdown would be unbearable for everyone. When we started to look into her reactions and what the triggers might be, we began to see that extreme anxiety was driving a lot of what happened.

It does not feel easy to describe the ways in which Sasha was different to her older sister. I was always aware of how, when I explained Sasha's reactions, it came across as if she was being selfish, or naughty. But it was more than that; it was as if her will was being driven by something entirely different to Tamsin. She never responded to any incentives or rewards such as stickers or treats, and she always did things only on her own terms. We knew we could always make Tamsin do anything we wanted her to – by this I mean everyday activities like homework, going shopping or visiting family and friends. Tamsin responded well to typical parenting methods such as reward systems, or praise, or consequences, and she simply knew and accepted that we were in charge. Sasha did not show any signs of understanding this. She showed virtually no respect for anyone in authority, but not in a rude or intentional way. If she had decided she was not going to go out of the house, we simply could not change her mind or make her go. It was quite an isolating experience when she was younger. Leaving the house to go anywhere other than swimming or the local farm village she knew well became virtually impossible for a while. Toddler groups were a definite no-go as previously mentioned, because Sasha seemed unable to follow instructions and join in.

The thought ran through my mind on more than one occasion that if there was a need to leave the house for an urgent issue, to take Tamsin to hospital for example, and Sasha refused to go, I might have to find a physical strength I had never used before to get Sasha into the car. But I also understood that there was not much point exerting that kind of force to simply go shopping on an average day, as the ensuing meltdown would most definitely ensure that no useful shopping would be achieved. So, I altered my parenting style and thought carefully when making decisions about where we would go and what we would do.

It felt like we were permanently walking on eggshells. We learnt how to manage life by using different approaches that took into account her needs, but it did mean that Sasha appeared to be the one always in control. A report we received about Sasha in those days reinforced this view when it stated, 'Sasha has subtle control most of the time.' I liked to tell myself that it was me who was actually the one in control, because I was the one making decisions about what we would or wouldn't attempt, but of course I would not have needed to make those choices if Sasha had not reacted in an extreme manner. I tended not to make fixed plans as I was never quite sure what mood Sasha would be in on any given day. We needed a purpose and Sasha's agreement for a day out; a meeting in the park with friends could work occasionally, but we would most likely only be there for ten minutes before Sasha decided she had had enough and it was time to leave. And once she had decided, there was no changing her mind. I became accustomed to thinking about every minor detail that might lead to an outing being successful or not – what time of the day to travel, what kind of transport to use, food and drink options, who would be there, how long we would be out for, what weather was expected, quick escape routes, what to take with us. All aspects that a typical parent might consider fleetingly, but we had to consider all options exhaustively to make sure the day would work for Sasha. We knew that we didn't need this level of planning to leave the house with only our eldest daughter. It was on a different level.

A few months after our PDA lightbulb moment we went back for Sasha's six-monthly check with the paediatrician. We brought up the subject of PDA, asking whether this new information we had discovered might relate to Sasha, but it was suggested that it might not help Sasha to have PDA as a diagnosis. We were told that PDA could not be diagnosed anyway because it was not officially listed in the medical manuals. At the time we did not understand that comment, but after the appointment we did some more research. The medical manuals referred to were the ICD (International Statistical Classification of Diseases and Related Health Problems, a medical classification list published by the World Health Organization), and the DSM (Diagnostic and Statistical Manual of Mental Disorders, published by the American Psychiatric Association (APA) for the classification of mental disorders). These publications have now reached their 11th (ICD) and 5th (DSM) versions.

PDD-NOS and other terms were replaced with the overriding term of autism spectrum disorder (ASD) in the most recent versions of the main diagnostic manuals, but many people, including me, do not like the word disorder. I do not think autism should be described as a disease or a mental disorder as that implies something wrong. I view autism as a difference in how the brain thinks and works. It is worth noting that understanding of how unique and different we all are is improving all the time, and with that more changes in terminology will come. Just because PDA is not currently listed as a separate condition within these manuals does not mean individuals with these characteristics do not exist. Language choice is so important and I am sure that discussions around this are ongoing.

A year or so after the initial autism diagnosis we decided to ask for Sasha to be referred to somewhere else that would diagnose PDA. We specifically asked to go to the Elizabeth Newson Centre in Nottingham because we knew they were specialists in PDA. Due to the way healthcare funding works in our county, we were told that being referred to Nottingham was not possible but that we could be referred to a specialist autism clinic at Great Ormond Street Hospital (GOSH) in London.

When we received our appointment with the team at GOSH, Sasha was six years old. I remember feeling a little nervous before the appointment as I was not sure what to expect. I also did not think I would ever be able to get Sasha to agree to go to the hospital as it would be a journey that would take around an hour, involving travel by car, train and bus. I rejoiced when I found out that there was a McDonalds enroute; fries turned out to be a great incentive, pretty much the only one that has ever worked for Sasha (but even then, they don't always work). The whole family went to this initial appointment at GOSH. It was held in a small stuffy room, and we were all asked lots of questions about how life with Sasha had been up to that point. They tried to talk to Sasha directly, but she wouldn't respond to them at all. I knew this to be sheer anxiety from the unusual situation rather than petulance or defiance. We were told a further appointment would be necessary, to undergo some in-depth questioning, and I wondered what we had let ourselves in for. Seven months later we were invited back, with an indication that the appointment would take two-and-a-half hours, and that it would involve a lot of talking and questions for us all. I actually didn't think Sasha would agree to stay longer than ten minutes but I was prepared to give it a shot as we were so keen to understand her better.

This time Sasha's dad and I were interviewed in one room while Sasha was taken off by a psychologist to another room, to do some 'playing'. What the psychologist was actually trying to do was complete two sets of testing – cognitive testing to assess Sasha's abilities and another ADOS test. Sasha was brought back to see us after the first hour and I could instantly tell she wasn't happy. She reluctantly agreed to return to the room with the psychologist after a short break though and surprisingly ended up staying there for a further two hours. Towards the end of that time, they returned to our room again, and the psychologist asked if I would sit in with them to try to get the last answers completed. By that point Sasha was extremely tired though, and in full-blown avoidance mode. Her head was on the table and she was deliberately not listening. She blocked out the questions with noise or her hands over her ears, saying she couldn't do it because her 'energy had gone'.

It transpired that Sasha had only given answers to half of the first test in the time she was away from us. In three hours, she had only agreed to do what most other children would finish in about 45 minutes. I think the psychologist was almost as exhausted as Sasha after trying to persuade her to cooperate. To be honest, the thought that ran through my mind at that point was 'try doing this every day and then see how you feel'.

On a serious note, I felt that what had happened was both good and bad. Good in that they did get to see the 'real' Sasha and could appreciate that we were not making up how difficult she could be, but on the other hand not good that they couldn't actually complete the testing. I do remember feeling bizarrely proud about the fact that Sasha scored much higher than her peer group generally would for one part of the tests. That was the one session of the test she did agree to complete fully, called the non-verbal reasoning section, where they showed her pictures and would question around them to try and assess what she could understand or infer from them.

On a subsequent visit Sasha did actually manage a full hour of a speech and language assessment, albeit with us parents in the room aiding and encouraging her. The speech therapist was very pleased with the results, stating that her language memory score placed her in the top 12 per cent of typically developing children of her age. We made one final visit with Sasha a few months later so the psychologists could try to complete some more of the original cognitive tests. We remained in the room with Sasha again that time, but it was another difficult day in terms of cooperation. When we received our detailed reports at the end of this experience, the team did admit that most children they see are at least willing to try the tests, even if they are not able to answer the questions. Not so for our girl. Sasha avoided completing most of their tests, reinforcing the ideas we had formed about Pathological Demand Avoidance.

We received some very detailed reports about Sasha six months later, confirming that the original diagnosis of autism definitely applied. The staff in this clinic at Great Ormond Street had told us at the very first meeting that, like our paediatrician, they also would not diagnose PDA specifically. At the end of the process, however, they did verbally agree with our thoughts on PDA being a good fit for Sasha. We were disappointed to not walk away from the whole experience with a PDA confirmation in black and white, but as we understood it, this was down to ongoing discussions over whether PDA could be recognized as a formal diagnosis. More research is still needed but there are clinicians around the UK who do recognize this profile of autism and who will diagnose it. After receiving the GOSH reports, our paediatrician added a second line to Sasha's official diagnosis, acknowledging Pathological Demand Avoidance behaviours. We made a conscious decision not to put Sasha through the stress of any further assessments.

When I look back over the numerous reports that we received over the nursery and infant school years, similar messages were repeated throughout. These only served to confirm our thoughts about PDA. They stated that Sasha had social communication difficulties in keeping with her diagnosis of autism, but also that she was 'generally happy provided she was not being asked to do something not of her choosing'. It was noted that triggers to her behaviour appeared to include engaging in adult-directed tasks, difficulties understanding the language of others, difficulties with expressing herself and changes to her routine. Further comments were made such as: 'At times there appears to be no specific triggers to her behaviour, although it frequently appears to have the function of gaining control of her environment. She sometimes curls up into a ball when distressed, and at these times she refuses to uncurl.'

At school there were differing opinions about the term Pathological Demand Avoidance, both in terms of whether it was a 'real' diagnosis and, if it was, whether it related to our girl. When I read the book *Understanding Pathological Demand Avoidance Syndrome in Children*, I had tears in my eyes because it felt like the writers were describing my child in great detail.[2] I took a copy of this book into school in the hope that staff would read it and understand why Sasha reacted in the way she did. Of course, now I have come to realize that school staff are generally much too busy to be reading specialist textbooks, so a short summary of the condition might have been more useful. But at the time I was blown away by how the book seemed to have been written about Sasha, even though it wasn't. It helped me understand our daughter more and I thought others would find it helpful too, if they read the book. Whilst I am sure that some staff did read the book or at least flick through it, I know that there were others who refused to entertain the idea of PDA at all. I suspect they are unlikely to be reading this book either, which is a shame! But from that point on I always knew that there would be those who believed in PDA and those who did not. Somewhere around the middle though, there are many people who may have been brought up with traditional parenting or teaching styles, and for some of them it may take a while for the idea of PDA to sink in. There are plenty of people who instinctively 'get it' and who just want to do their best to help children whatever the diagnosis or need, and I am extremely grateful for them.

After a period of living with Sasha refusing and avoiding all sorts of situations, we realized that it wasn't a case of her consciously choosing to do what she wanted to, and refusing the boring stuff or what she did not want to do. It wasn't about 'want' at all. A phrase often used to help others understand PDA is 'can't help won't'. That is to say, PDA individuals can't help the fact that they won't do something. It is not a deliberate choice to benefit themselves; there are underlying reasons and an inability to comply.

---

2   Phil Christie, Ruth Fidler, Zara Healy and Margot Duncan (2011) *Understanding Pathological Demand Avoidance Syndrome in Children.* London: Jessica Kingsley Publishers.

At times even activities which Sasha loved to do, such as going swimming, or activities she desperately wanted to do, like join a gymnastics club, became too much of a demand and she could not make it out of the house for them. Of course, it wasn't always all about the demand; often there were other factors at play, such as sensory issues, but there were definite times when she avoided the demand simply because it was a demand. Because it was phrased in the wrong way. Or because she had already faced too many demands that day and this one last thing tipped the balance. An old saying that springs to mind is that it seemed as if our girl would 'cut her nose off to spite her face'. We were not forcing her to do something she loved like going swimming, we simply suggested it because we thought she would enjoy it. She would want to do the activity, but would then find herself unable to because of the demand involved.

I have been asked if PDA is real. It certainly feels very real in our house. Most people, autistic or not, can experience demand avoidance. Toddlers, children, teenagers and adults – lots of us avoid doing things when they are unpleasant or not fun. Or we might procrastinate when we have something to do that we find hard (revising, housework, writing a book!). This is not the same as Pathological Demand Avoidance. So, what is the difference? In order to understand PDA better we first need to consider what a demand actually is, and why this might cause a problem. Demands are not just when we are specifically told or asked to do something, they can also include unspoken expectations, such as societal demands or patterns. Sitting at a table to eat food is a demand, being expected to be polite to others is a demand, getting to appointments on time, producing work, completing all stages of a video game, leaving the house to go and do something fun are all demands. The list of demands in the daily life of an adult is considerable and even longer for children who are constantly being told what to do.

PDA individuals struggle to do things if they perceive them to be a demand. They avoid not only unpleasant tasks, but activities they actually want to do. Normal, everyday tasks that others might find mundane but easy, like washing themselves, getting dressed or going to bed, can be a challenge for PDAers, but they might also avoid what seems like fun to others. Hiding or fleeing or exploding and not being able to take part in activities is a result of anxiety. On top of this are the demands that PDA individuals place upon themselves, including trying to live up to their own expectations of what they believe they should be achieving.

I am often asked how I have the strength to be so positive and I reply that I feel lucky. Lucky that I have two daughters who are both so very different (and who I love equally, of course). Because we were able to parent our eldest daughter in a typical style, we could clearly see the differences in reactions from Sasha when we tried similar parenting methods with her. We were lucky that Sasha was assessed at an early age by a skilled paediatrician and that she recognized the signs of autism. We were lucky to stumble across descriptions of Pathological Demand Avoidance early on because this gave us confidence in our parenting and the knowledge that we needed to approach everything differently. And we have been lucky in having support and understanding from our wonderful family and friends.

At this point, I would like to thank the PDA Society for being a lifeline for me in the early days; I have used their comprehensive website as a great source for lots of information about PDA and I know they have helped countless other families too. Everyone involved with the PDA Society works hard behind the scenes to support others, and their work with clinicians and input into further research on PDA is invaluable. Through their forum I chatted with many families whose children would react in the same way that

Sasha did, and it gave me comfort to know that it wasn't just me. In the years that followed I became a Trainer for the PDA Society, to help other families find out more about this condition that was rarely heard of or spoken about. It still gives me great pleasure to help support other families and educate professionals because I know that judgement often comes from a place of ignorance and fear. I believe that society will become more welcoming and inclusive if more people understand, and I hope that sharing information will help smooth the way to a brighter future for our daughter and others who find life difficult because of demands, expectations and inflexible attitudes.

ADVICE FOR PARENTS AND CARERS

- Consider the list of PDA characteristics and whether they apply to your child. Demand avoidance is common for many children, autistic or not, when it comes to doing things that take them out of a comfort zone. PDA is more than that. Pathological Demand Avoidance occurs on an everyday basis and can prevent PDAers from doing even what might seem to be enjoyable activities.

- PDA children grow up to be PDA adults. Although the demands of school disappear after a certain age, many of the same everyday demands still exist, along with some new challenges of adult life. Age and experience can mean that new coping strategies are learnt, however. I highly recommend searching out the PDA adults who have shared their stories as they have many helpful insights that parents and carers of younger PDA children can learn from.

- A diagnosis can be helpful in terms of receiving further support from others, but the biggest way in which you can help a PDA child is by taking the time to understand their challenges. Altering our own behaviour and expectations helps to build a trusting relationship with them.

- The PDA Society website is the best, most up-to-date source for information about PDA. If you can't find the answer to a question there then there is an enquiry line where volunteers with experience can help by giving advice around more specific situations.

Chapter 3
THE EARLY YEARS: BIRTH TO AGE FIVE

have been asked many times about what Sasha was like when she was young, before she received the autism diagnosis. Were there any signs? Was her behaviour unusual? Did we suspect anything? The speech delay was an obvious flag, but until we reached the point of having that checked out, there were no other concerns. For the first few months after her birth, Sasha seemed quite content. I would have described her as an easy baby, as much as any baby could be described in that way. Life began to get slightly more difficult when she passed the six-month stage though. I started taking Tamsin, who was by then two-and-a-half years old, to toddler groups such as music sessions and dance classes, and of course Sasha needed to come with us. If it was over a nap time for Sasha the activity might go well, but if not, and if Sasha did not want to be there, she would let us know, loudly. Tamsin seemed to enjoy sitting down, listening and following instructions as part of a group, but Sasha rarely appeared to be happy when in an organized group with others.

When Tamsin started attending nursery more frequently I tried to take Sasha to some toddler sessions of her own, choosing activities I thought she would enjoy rather than those that had suited her sister. Sasha could not sit still and listen to instructions though;

instead, she preferred to run around and do her own thing, not paying attention to the teachers or group leaders. It seemed as if she didn't recognize that the teacher was in charge or that she should be joining in with the group. I can still picture the scene and hear the loud noise of her shoes on the wooden floor in one large hall as she ran the full length of it, up and down, over and over, next to where all the other parents and children were sitting quietly in a circle on the carpet. Although I tried to tell her to sit down with me, she wasn't listening. It was like she was in a world of her own and not aware that the others were trying to listen to the music teacher. I was embarrassed, and after a while I felt that I couldn't continue taking her to those types of sessions because the behaviour was disruptive to others. I used to put her behaviour down to hunger or tiredness, but it happened so often that I knew it was beginning to sound like a lame excuse. I assumed the other parents were blaming my parenting and thinking I should just be stricter with her.

Some of my earliest vivid memories of unusual or 'extreme' behaviour came from the summer just after Sasha turned two. This was a couple of months before her first speech assessment, and well before the autism diagnosis. We drove to France on holiday via Eurotunnel and all started off well. As we left the tunnel having reached France, there was a big queue of slow-moving traffic to exit the terminal area. Sasha began to get distressed, fighting to get out of her car seat, but we weren't able to stop the car anywhere. Before long she had literally screamed herself sick because she didn't want to be trapped in the car seat. We eventually managed to find somewhere to pull over and had to wait a long time for her to properly calm down. We then continued our journey, making a planned overnight stop at a small hotel, on the way to our final destination in France. Tamsin was tired and ready to sleep, but Sasha was still wide awake. In an attempt to settle Sasha to sleep, I took her out in the pushchair. Despite the fact that we had never been in that town or country before, Sasha was very definite about the route she wanted me to push her along. If I tried to walk a way she wasn't happy with, she would scream and get very agitated. She would try to direct me by pointing towards specific roads, even though she had no idea where she was or where they were heading to. When I followed her lead, she would become calm again.

I realized this kind of 'directing' was happening on a regular basis at home too. Routine seemed to suit Sasha some days, although on others it did not seem to be so important. If I tried to walk her to nursery on a different day, at a different time or via a different route, it could often lead to a meltdown. Once upset, the only way to settle her was to retrace our steps, go back to the beginning and start again. The same occasionally happened if we travelled somewhere in the car. Sasha would suddenly become upset but we wouldn't know why. We sometimes wondered if Sasha had maybe been expecting to go somewhere else. Not having the language to explain what was upsetting her must have been incredibly frustrating for Sasha, but it also made it pretty difficult for us to figure out what the problem was.

After the autism diagnosis I tried to take Sasha along to a couple of activity sessions that were advertised specifically for children with additional needs, but those groups were generally attended by children with much higher care needs. I felt like a fraud, as if I was accessing a resource that my child did not actually need, because to everyone else it must have appeared as though Sasha was quite happy and capable as long as she was left alone, with whatever she wanted to hand. Eventually I reached a point where I mostly stayed home with Sasha. There I knew she was comfortable, content in surroundings she loved, with things that made her happy. Having my undivided attention when she needed it suited her better too and she seemed calmer overall.

Sasha was very affectionate with people she knew, especially family and our friends. She could be wary of strangers but on some occasions had no fear or nerves and would approach and talk to anyone. When I went to meet up with friends in the park, I rarely got a chance to sit and chat with them because Sasha would quite happily walk away from where I was. She would keep walking, without looking back, and I would have to go after her. It wasn't always obvious to us where she was heading or what she was trying to get to, but she would seem very determined to be somewhere else, doing something else. Tamsin, on the other hand, always wanted to be by my side. She would sit happily on a picnic blanket and stay there, playing with toys or looking at books, for as long as I was there.

From around the age of nine months old, Sasha began attending nursery sessions at a small setting near our home. Initially this was only one session a week, for a couple of hours at a time. We had decided to sign her up for these sessions because her older sister was already enjoying spending time at that particular nursery and we thought it would be a good idea for Sasha to also spend a short amount of time away from home, to get her used to socializing with other children and adults. At this stage, we assumed Sasha was developing typically because her behaviour had given us no cause for concern. Although she seemed quite happy to go into nursery, we did have a few problems getting her to settle there. Sometimes I would have to go into the nursery building myself, partway through a session, to give her a bottle of milk before she would settle to sleep at nap times with the other children. She refused to be settled by the nursery staff. It didn't feel like a big issue at the time, but when I think back now, I don't remember seeing any other parents having to do that for their children.

Sasha carried on with just one session a week at the nursery for the following year, and over this time she progressed from the baby room into a toddler room, where the children were becoming more

active. At home we hadn't experienced any problems or noticed anything unusual, but when she was around 18 months old, the nursery
staff began to gently raise some concerns over Sasha's development.
They told us that Sasha didn't always respond to her own name, or to
any other source of sound such as a car, or knock on the door, or the
phone ringing. She very rarely maintained attention on any activity,
and she didn't seem to respond to facial expressions of emotion.
None of this caused any great concern though and we assumed that
Sasha would catch up to her peers in good time.

We were asked to fill in a series of checklists called 'a guide to
individual assessment of early learning and development'. These
checklists covered seven key areas: play and early learning skills,
expressive speech and language skills, receptive language skills, fine
motor skills, gross motor skills, self-help and independence, and
social and emotional development. When completed, the reports
showed that at the age of 19 months, Sasha's fine and gross motor
skills were all good and developing typically. The most noticeable
delays picked out from the checklists at this age were in the areas of
expressive and receptive language skills, and social and emotional
development. When looking at the suggested age relevant actions
for these categories, Sasha appeared to be around six months behind
her peers in terms of development. In the play and early learning
and self-help and independent skills categories, there were some
scattered checkpoints that she hadn't quite reached. Sasha had not
begun to use role play at this stage and her general play did seem different in some ways to how our older daughter had been. We often
found long lines of objects that Sasha had created around the house
– DVD cases, books, cushions, dolls, Playmobil characters, plastic
play food pieces or other random items. One day after leaving Sasha
alone to play for just a short while, I walked out of the kitchen to
find a line of shoes stretching from the under stairs cupboard all the
way upstairs and into a bedroom! Outside in the garden there were

always lines of stones or piles of leaves and at Christmas time Sasha stretched all the presents out in one long line before even thinking about unwrapping them. Taking photos of this kind of behaviour proved useful as an indication of how her actions were somewhat different to many other children of this age.

We were beginning to notice other differences between Sasha's behaviour and how our older daughter had acted at a similar age. If Tamsin or other children were upset Sasha didn't seem to show concern for them, but instead would become upset herself. When out and about she had no sense of fear and would run away from us without stopping to look back, despite being told to stop and wait. She sometimes ran straight onto a road, and thought nothing of stopping and sitting down in the middle of a road if she had decided she didn't want to go any further. Although we attempted toilet training at the usual age for toddlers, Sasha didn't appear to grasp the concept at first. We stopped trying and waited almost a year, until we felt that Sasha did understand what we were trying to achieve. I remember at that stage we tried to encourage her into the toilet room by giving her new toys to hold when she agreed to sit without her nappy on the toilet, but this only worked a couple of times and then she resolutely refused to even enter the toilet room. She didn't appear scared or anxious of it in any way, it just seemed as if she didn't want to do it and so that was that. She preferred to use a potty in whichever room she was in. She would not wash her hands herself and always put up a fight if she saw a toothbrush, something that hasn't changed over the years! She tended to be slightly rough with belongings and would sometimes throw an item if frustrated because it didn't work the way she wanted it to, but she was never aggressive towards us or others. She didn't seem to learn from consequences in the same way our older daughter had, and she didn't have the same instinct for what was right or wrong in terms of behaviour. I would have to clear up after Sasha constantly, in a way that I hadn't needed to for Tamsin; play dough or sand scattered all around a room and wiped on the arms of sofas, pen drawings on furniture and carpets and too much toilet roll piled up in the toilet would all happen repeatedly. It didn't matter how many times I tried to tell Sasha no, or to talk to her about the error of her ways, she just never seemed to understand or learn from the experience. Of course, lots of young children are prone to creating a mess, but the difference was that in our house these kinds of actions carried on well past the age that typical toddlers would 'explore' with this kind of behaviour.

Sasha struggled a lot with the concept of time when she was younger. She wouldn't attempt to talk to us, or let us talk to her, about any event which had happened in the past, and we were not able to refer even in simple terms to an event which had happened that day. She didn't ever have a two-way conversation with us back then. If we told her that her grandparents were arriving tomorrow she would get very excited and expect them to be there instantly and then get very confused and upset when she realized they were not there. If we ever wanted to leave the house to go somewhere as a family, we had to quietly make sure that we were all ready ourselves first before we got Sasha ready, because as soon as Sasha was ready she wanted to leave. She was never happy to sit and wait for others. My mum had a phrase that she often repeated to me and my brothers as we were growing up: 'Patience is a virtue.' Sasha did not seem able to be patient, ever.

Sasha rarely focused on one activity for any length of time. She would flit from one toy to another and liked watching DVDs of her favourite television shows. Dora, Teletubbies and Peppa Pig were the favourite characters on repeat, but plenty of others were enjoyed and revisited from time to time. Many other toddlers might behave in this way, but Sasha was different in that she would skip forwards or backwards to specific parts of the shows that she wanted to watch over and over again rather than sit and watch the whole DVD all the way through. She also watched CBeebies on the television at times, but she was very particular about which programmes she would listen to. She was always happier if the television was permanently on as background noise, but she was often doing other activities and sometimes it didn't appear as if she was actually watching the programmes. But we came to realize that she was always listening and she remembered nearly everything. *Waybuloo* and *Numberjacks* were two of her favourite shows, and *Same Smile* and *Mighty Mites* were others that were often on repeat. We would record them so she could watch at any time of the day, but then she would request specific episodes from these series such as 'the beach one' or 'the bowling one'. If we couldn't find the requested episodes immediately for her on the recorded programmes list, she would quickly become extremely upset and agitated.

Sasha was not interested in books at all, and to this day she will still tell everyone that she dislikes them. In the early years we tried to read books to her as part of a bedtime routine, just as we had for our eldest, but Sasha refused them all and pushed us away. After a couple of years of this she did eventually reluctantly let us read to her, but only the stories she wanted to hear. The book choice had to come from her; if we picked one up and suggested it to her she would reject it. Sometimes she insisted we omit certain paragraphs or even whole pages from the books she chose; she would make us flick through pages in double-quick time and then stop us at only the pages she wanted to hear. At some point Sasha decided that she was going to read the books to me herself. She couldn't actually read but would say something out loud in her own cute way for every single page, followed by saying 'The End' for the last page. Eventually, after a couple more years of page flipping and general fooling around at bedtime, she did end up letting me read most of the words in any book to her, which was a pleasant change. It still had to be only the books she chose though. She preferred it if I acted the fool when reading, using silly voices and accents, but would get upset if I used a serious voice. I think Sasha's speech developed at a faster rate when she started to let more books be read to her. It felt like her understanding and use of language began to approach the levels of her peers. The sounds were still largely unclear but we hoped that those would improve over the following year, in time for her 'big' school start in Reception class.

Sasha was an active little girl and she had no difficulties with walking, running or climbing, although she didn't choose to climb very often. For some unknown reason, she seemed to develop a fear of going down slides at some point in her early years after enjoying them initially. She always enjoyed swings and roundabouts though. Swimming was an activity she really loved; being in a pool always made her happy. For several months when she was around three or four, I remember feeling worried that she might refuse to ever swim again because she had developed a specific extreme anxiety about how her fingers became wrinkly in the water. In both swimming pool and bath, she would spend a long time having fun in the water but then end up staring at her wrinkly fingers and frantically trying to rub them smooth again. It was almost painful to see her so upset about it and not be able to 'fix' it for her. We tried swimming lessons but they did not go well. Sasha was not keen on following instructions and learning actual swimming techniques, she just wanted to splash around and have fun in her own way. Over the years which followed she taught herself how to swim at her own pace. It took her several months to overcome her anxiety about getting her face wet, but we knew there was no point in pushing her to do it any faster or we might have risked her not wanting to return to a pool at all. Now she is like a mermaid in the water! She did it in her own time, and on her own terms. That has been the key to most of her successes, to be honest.

Nine weeks after the autism diagnosis we were visited at home by two specialists from the Autism Advisory Service. They listened to our experiences of how Sasha behaved and then assessed her using an ADOS test (Autism Diagnostic Observation Schedule). The ADOS for young children is a play-based assessment that uses semi-structured role-play type questions to see if there are any difficulties with social communication, interaction or restricted repetitive behaviours. Those carrying out an ADOS might typically look for use of eye contact, a range of facial expressions to communicate feelings, unusual language use, and sensory behaviours such as licking or sniffing. Each part of the assessment is scored, and if a certain score is reached then autism is diagnosed. It is worth noting that for some children, both girls and boys and particularly PDAers, symptoms can be camouflaged, which means that they may not score highly in the ADOS. For Sasha, eye contact did not ever seem to be a problem, and in the right situation, with little pressure on her, and if she was in the right mood, she would come across as being very sociable and able to express and understand emotion. As detailed before, her speech sounds and use of language were not typical of other children her age though, and the sensory issues were easy to spot by this stage.

It was agreed that we would begin to receive a weekly visit from an Early Years Autism Specialist (the EYAS), who would try to work with Sasha to teach her skills that she hadn't seemed to grasp, such as reciprocal play. We were told the visits would take place in term-time only, and I remember my initial thoughts were how strange it was that anyone would think that a child's difficulties would suddenly disappear in the holidays. The sessions were only an hour long each week, but they made a huge difference to my life at the time. By this stage it had become extremely difficult to leave the house with Sasha and I was alone at home with her most days, so the chance for her to try to interact with anybody else was very welcome. The paediatrician's report after our first meeting had confirmed that Sasha was quite a happy little girl, as long as she wasn't being asked to do something that was not of her own choosing. The EYAS tried to engage Sasha during these sessions by offering to play a variety of games with her. The games were specially designed for early years children, to try to teach patience, give and take, and language skills. It took a few weeks for Sasha to accept a stranger coming into our house to talk to her, but once some trust had been built up, Sasha did indeed begin to engage in the games. But only the ones she was interested in. If the EYAS tried to push Sasha to play one she wasn't keen on, Sasha would refuse or shut down completely. There were quite a few occasions when it was clear that Sasha had reached the limit of interacting. Her way of opting out was to run upstairs to her bedroom and pull the duvet up over herself, pretending she had gone to sleep. If Sasha had become very upset with how the session was going, she would be drained from the emotion and would actually fall asleep. It only took a few months of these visits before Sasha realized that she was always being pushed to do more, and the relationship began to slide downhill. I was grateful for the attempts made though, and also had a feeling of relief that another person was seeing the kind of behaviours that I experienced daily. This was confirmation that we were not bad parents, and it was not a case of us not being able to teach our little girl the basics. Another adult had also tried and not succeeded. In some strange kind of way, I felt vindicated.

In the summer of 2010, a few months after the autism diagnosis, we were accepted onto a local EarlyBird Parent Programme being run on behalf of the National Autistic Society. This was a course for the parents of autistic, preschool age children, and the aim was to help us learn ways to support our children and cope with various behaviours. The course ran for 12 weeks and we shared weekly group sessions with four other couples whose children had also recently received a diagnosis of autism.

The programme included visits from the course leaders to our home settings, to video us all with our children. The idea was that we could then share the challenges we were facing with others in the group, and that hopefully over time we would all see improvements in the way we handled situations at home. During the first home visit, Sasha was on top form. She was very chatty and bubbly with the two strangers initially, but as soon as they started videoing her, she stopped still in front of the television and ignored them. I felt that wouldn't be a fair representation of Sasha so I tried to get her attention back, suggesting she sing Twinkle Twinkle Little Star. She replied no, but then retorted cheekily with a suggestion of Baa Baa Black Sheep! I ended up singing that on my own though, because despite that song being her choice, she then refused to join in. Sasha was still in a good mood though, and it was lovely to capture that because we knew that was a good representation of Sasha's personality, most of the time. Happy as long as nobody was forcing her to do something she did not want to do.

The EarlyBird course helped us understand autism better and it was a real lifeline in those early days. What was particularly helpful was that it involved attending as a couple, meaning partners were included and information was heard first-hand by both parties rather than having to be relayed later at home. For both me and Sasha's dad to be out of the house at the same time, leaving someone else to look after the girls, felt almost impossible at that stage, mostly because we didn't believe anyone else could understand Sasha and accommodate her different needs. We never felt able to use babysitters for Sasha, but family and close friends offered to help out so we could attend this course, which we were very grateful for.

A few months later I attended another parent course; this one was provided by Hanen and called More Than Words. It aimed to help parents to create everyday opportunities to improve their child's communication skills. I found this one slightly less useful than the EarlyBird course as Sasha was already using more spoken language than most of the children of other parents attending. I went on to attend more courses over the years, and although some were quite generic about autism and the suggested strategies did not seem to work for our daughter, I nearly always learnt something new. An extra snippet of information or another parent's shared experience pointed me in the right direction. However, 13 years after our daughter's diagnosis, I was surprised to be invited to a parenting course by some practitioners. The implication that I did not know what I was doing by that stage both tickled and exasperated me! I recommend that parents ask around for advice from other families about which courses have provided the most helpful information. Speaking with others who truly understand the unique challenges posed by PDA can lead to finding lifelong friends and a great support network.

By the autumn of 2010, 12 months after the first speech and language therapy assessment, Sasha was reported to be presenting with only a mild speech and language delay. This felt like a huge improvement on the first report that had suggested a severe expressive and receptive language delay, and we were relieved that progress had been made. A report provided by the nursery around that time stated, 'Sasha is generally happy at nursery and confident in her surroundings. She can enjoy activities, particularly creative messy ones, but this is very mood dependent.' On the blog I wrote that Sasha was up and down in mood; quite happy and bubbly most days but always 'high maintenance' at the same time.

Sasha's behaviour became more problematic for the staff at

nursery though. Sasha appeared quite happy to go to the nursery but there were a lot of meltdowns once she was there, for seemingly small and sometimes difficult to understand reasons. These included examples such as her sunhat not being on quite right, not having the colour cup she liked, other children trying to play with what she was using, not wanting to clear up pencils or toys after she had been using them or not wanting to put her shoes and socks on. One afternoon when I walked in to collect Sasha from the nursery, I found her fast asleep, face down on a cushion with her jacket on, looking very hot and bothered. I was informed that she had got upset when they were about to take the class out for a walk, because she would not hold someone's hand. It wasn't clear whether they had been trying to get her to hold the hand of a staff member or the hand of another child, but with all the other parents filing in behind me to collect their children, I didn't feel I could ask too many questions. The staff just told me they were not able to take her out because she had got so upset and would not calm down. Sasha had had a huge meltdown and burned herself out. She didn't wake when I lifted her up, and she had a scratch on her nose, possibly from her own fingernails when she was distressed. It made me feel sad; nobody likes to think of their child as being upset when they are not there to comfort them. Sasha must have had her own reasons for not wanting to hold hands but she was unable to communicate them. She was not being intentionally awkward or difficult.

Many of the daily reports I received around that time included mention of Sasha getting upset, lying on the floor crying, refusing to move or refusing to join in with different activities. Nursery staff liked to take the children out in groups for a walk most days to the park in the area where the nursery was located, close to our home, but Sasha often point blank refused to go out with them. With no extra funding available for extra support for Sasha, staff at the nursery felt they were not able to manage her as part of their group any longer and she was not offered a full-time place for the preschool year. It was time for us to try something else.

We held an emergency meeting at the nursery and everyone involved agreed that it would be better if Sasha moved on to a different setting where there might be more support for her. We chose the nursery that was attached to the Infant school that her older sister was already attending. The staff there were warm and welcoming and assured us that they could be flexible for Sasha. We knew she would be given a place in the Reception class there the following September anyway, so it was agreed the transition to the new setting might as well take place sooner rather than later.

Education, Health and Care Plan

That meeting with the nursery staff was the point at which it dawned on me that Sasha receiving a diagnosis was not going to be the hard part of our 'journey'. The difficult times would be what followed – striving to ensure the best future possible for our daughter, battling against the general lack of understanding, and fighting for funding. I quickly realized that I needed to grow an extra thick skin overnight. I have always considered myself to be a fairly calm and rational person, but I was not confident and I did not like conflict. I did not relish the thought of the new role I was being thrust into, being 'that' parent who stood out from the crowd. Having a child who is different to the majority, one who needs extra support, can lead to confrontation and difficult conversations. I knew that I needed to let others know about what worked for Sasha because I had seen the difference it made when I paid attention to the little things. I somehow found an inner strength and determination to do what was right for Sasha and to not worry about what others thought of me.

The reports provided by the original nursery made it clear that Sasha would require extra support in school. We didn't know how much support, what kind of support, or how to go about applying for this support, but after some research and speaking with other parents locally we found out that we would need to ask the Local Authority to undertake an assessment of Sasha's educational needs. Their assessment and reports would determine whether Sasha would be awarded a Statement of Special Educational Needs, a document that should detail what support she needed. Reforms of the education system for children and young people with additional educational needs took place a few years later, and this document is now known as an Education, Health and Care Plan (EHCP) in England.

I am going to take a little moment out here, to share my thoughts on the word 'special'. Special needs or special schools, neither phrase sits well with me. I don't want my daughter to get 'special' treatment, but I do know that she needs extra support and understanding for the challenges she faces every day. I think the word special was maybe originally introduced to somehow soften the way in which children with any kind of additional needs were talked about. Disabled or disability were viewed as bad words, and in the past those with disabilities were sadly assumed to be 'less than'. I believe attitudes have changed and this is thankfully no longer an accepted opinion, but it still seems hard to shake the use of the word special. What should we call schools that are not part of the mainstream group? Specialist? That may be considered a slightly better term but also brings up further thoughts and discussions around the idea of inclusion and leads to debate as to whether those with disabilities should always be educated alongside their peers rather than in separate settings. It is not my place to cover all of those issues in this book, but there are many writings on this topic that are worth diving into.

The EHCP application process involved us collecting reports and evidence to show why we felt there was a need for support for our daughter. We needed to complete a lengthy form consisting of lots of questions. It asked us to show how Sasha's diagnosis and difficulties impacted on her learning and development, and to give examples of support that had already been tried successfully or that didn't have the desired impact. It was emotionally draining to have to only write about the negatives of our fun-loving, happy girl, but we knew we had to document everything truthfully in order to ensure the correct help would be forthcoming.

Initially we were told off the record that Sasha 'wasn't bad enough' to be awarded any help. As someone who has worked with lots of parents of autistic children over the past few years, I can tell you now that this blanket statement is often made by those who should know better. It is not about being bad or good, or intelligent or not; it is about having needs over and above those of typically developing children. An EHCP is a legal document for any child or young person aged up to 25 who needs more support than is available in their current setting. It should identify needs and set out the additional support to meet those needs.

When I first applied for an EHCP for Sasha, there was a rumour going around that suggested having an EHCP was a bonus in some way, because it meant parents could choose which school their child attended. That was not the reason we applied for one; we were perfectly happy with the mainstream school we had already chosen. It is true that having an EHCP helped our daughter access some non-mainstream schools later on, but as I explain later, that didn't magically make those school environments suitable for our girl. What I liked about having an EHCP for Sasha though was the fact that, at least once a year, any professionals involved with Sasha would observe her in school and write a report, and after that we would get together as a group to discuss her progress and agree on the future actions.

Our first application for an assessment was turned down. I was not prepared to take no for an answer though, because I absolutely knew that Sasha would need more support in school than most of the other children. I followed up with everyone involved to make sure that enough evidence of Sasha's needs was provided and that the assessment would go ahead. I was told by more than one person that there were so many children receiving a diagnosis of autism that there were not enough resources to go round. It can be quite upsetting, when you enter this new world of educational needs and disabilities, to discover that hurdles and barriers to getting help are put in your path every step of the way. Very few people are there welcoming you, offering the support that you know your child needs. Local Authorities are run on budgets and it can feel like any child who needs more help than the average child is seen as a burden, both financially and in terms of effort.

Eventually, not long before Sasha was due to start her new nursery, the Local Authority did agree to assess her. An educational psychologist was sent into the school to observe Sasha and then wrote a summary of that visit, detailing what support Sasha would need. Next it was the turn of a speech and language therapist (SALT) to visit school and I remember smiling wryly at this news. As mentioned earlier in the book, it was a delay in Sasha's speech development that led us to the initial appointment with the paediatrician. We had been waiting for some help from the speech and language service ever since, but none had been forthcoming. We had employed a private speech therapist who had tried hard to engage Sasha, but found it difficult to work with her at that young age. With hindsight, hoping to persuade Sasha to sit still and repeat speech sounds at someone else's request was being somewhat optimistic. Instead, the private speech therapist tried some basic play therapy. As with most things where Sasha was concerned, that went well until it didn't! I found it interesting to review some of the early reports from the speech therapy service and the nursery, because they were peppered with phrases such as 'on her own terms', 'when motivated', 'may not engage at all in activities which do not interest her' and 'she may go off task and follow her own agenda at times when the language used is more complex or if she is not motivated to join in'. These are all phrases that I am sure will ring true for many parents of PDA children and which still apply to our girl today.

We realized that there would be fewer staff members to help Sasha at the new nursery. We were moving her from a place where there were only around six children to every one member of staff to a bigger setting where there were 30 children in a class with one teacher, one assistant and one nursery nurse. Sasha had been allocated a specific key worker at the first nursery, and from that we already knew that relationships were very important to Sasha. We also realized it took longer for her to become settled than most of the other children. I remember hoping that there would not be many other children with a high level of needs in the same class at the new nursery, because I felt sure that the assistants would be very stretched if that was the case.

The introductory session at the new nursery went better than I could have hoped for. In a way that appeared contrary to how autistic children were often described, Sasha seemed to thrive on novelty and the social factor of being around other people. This love of company seemed to apply to both adults and children; she did not seem to differentiate between them and she treated them all the same. In fact, as we had seen at the toddler sessions, it was almost as if Sasha did not see hierarchy; she did not realize that the teacher was in charge and she acted as if everyone were equal.

Sasha appeared to be in a good mood during that first day, but then her mood abruptly changed and she suddenly wanted to leave the nursery. She unusually agreed to tidy away the plastic food toys she had been playing with before we left – at home we had become accustomed to her leaving a trail of mess and not tidying anything away. Once the tidying was done and we were about to leave the room, another girl went over to start playing with that same play food and Sasha was not happy. I recall she ran across the room, shouting 'no' at the other girl, insisting she put the toys away again. To me it was obvious that Sasha was thinking the other girl was in the wrong; even though the session was still ongoing, Sasha had decided it was time to leave, so the other girl should too. To that other girl and her parents though, the reaction from Sasha probably seemed extreme and unnecessary. I remember leaving with the worry that others might consider our daughter's behaviour unreasonable.

If we watched Sasha closely, we could see there was usually a reason for her actions, but careful observation needed to happen a lot of the time to really understand what she was thinking or what the triggers to her behaviour were. When I took her to toddler groups in the early days, I was not able to chat to other parents there and relax, because I needed to be constantly aware of what was going on. Sasha found it difficult to share toys and any approach from other children could make her become very distressed. I had not needed to be so vigilant for our other daughter. Tamsin instinctively knew how she was expected to react to other children and adults. I would watch from a distance to make sure she was safe, but I felt comfortable to stand back and let her learn from interactions with others. That was a key difference between our girls I think; Tamsin was able to learn from mistakes made and move forwards but Sasha did not seem to be aware of the ways in which she acted and how that might be perceived by others. Of course, I would try to explain situations and provide suitable responses, but Sasha didn't seem to take any of it in and the same issues would crop up repeatedly.

I think the strong reaction from Sasha during the first nursery session was the first time, but not the last, where I worried that staff at school would think I was a parent who watched too closely and interfered too much. My one saving grace that kept me sane was the fact that Tamsin was already progressing well through the school. I had no need to keep a close eye on her; she was a child who liked to follow the rules and to do well. I rarely needed to speak with the teacher about her or discuss her needs in any way because I knew she was doing just fine. Tamsin was a complete opposite to Sasha; she was very aware of everything going on and she did not want to stick out in any way at all. Tamsin was quiet and well-behaved; Sasha was in no way *badly* behaved, but she was very definite about what she would or would not do, regardless of what was being asked of her. If she wasn't able to do something for any reason, there was no chance of persuading or gently encouraging her. School staff quickly came to realize that ways of motivating or teaching that might have worked for Tamsin and many other children simply did not work for Sasha.

The EHCP assessment process inched along slowly over the next few months while Sasha attended the new nursery. The speech and language report we were given after the first observation suggested that Sasha would need ten sessions of 90 minutes' duration each, spread across the academic year. It was highlighted to us that this was a huge amount of therapy in comparison to what some other children were getting, but in reality a lot of those allocated hours were to be used for report writing, attending meetings with school staff, and classroom observation. Very little time was to be spent working directly with Sasha. It began to dawn on us that little help was going to be offered by outside agencies, so I felt lucky to have found a school for our girls that was full of caring and supportive staff. Of course, when our eldest had started at that school, neither we, nor any of the people working there, had any idea that a large amount of extra input was going to be needed for our younger daughter. I feel hugely appreciative to this day that they showed such compassion and patience when it came to supporting Sasha. When the Statement was finally awarded, it confirmed that

Sasha would need extra support at the mainstream infant school, but it only mentioned small group work rather than detailing any amount of time for individual, one-to-one support. The staff were very understanding though, they listened to what I could tell them about Sasha's needs, and they were as flexible as they could be. They tried to involve her in everything that the other children did, as much as Sasha would allow them to.

While Sasha was in nursery I spent my time researching and then visiting some different types of educational settings. I think I had already subconsciously acknowledged that Sasha's demand avoidance was likely to be at odds with a school system full of demands. I also knew how important it was to watch her closely and understand the triggers for her frustration, and I knew this could prove difficult in a big class. In our county there are no schools specifically set up for autistic children, so instead I viewed a specialist provision for speech and language and a handful of other schools that were for children with moderate learning difficulties (MLD). The MLD schools were for children who were attaining below expected levels in many areas of the curriculum; in other words, children whose cognitive ability levels were some way below those of their peers. That didn't seem to apply for Sasha though, so we concluded that mainstream schooling was our only option.

Whilst researching other schools I heard of a specialist Early Years centre in our county, called TRACKS. Staff there were all experienced in supporting autistic children, and although the setting was a 20-mile drive from our house, I began to drive Sasha there once or twice a week. This gave her the chance of experiencing a safe new environment for a couple of hours, and because there was a higher ratio of staff to children, and a good understanding of each individual child's needs, I was able to leave Sasha there while I drove back home. That meant I would either get an hour to myself (usually spent catching up on housework of course!), or an hour to spend some quality time alone with our older daughter. That time was much appreciated and we could also see that in the quieter environment, Sasha was learning some new skills and improving her speech sounds.

When I reflect on these preschool years, I can see there were some indicators in terms of behaviour that backed up the autism diagnosis. Of course, the difference in speech and communication was an obvious factor, but there were other aspects too. Sasha acted like a typical toddler in some ways, but in others she seemed different. She needed constant input from either the television or her DVDs, in a way that her older sister had not. Her imaginative play was delayed; I would say it started around six months later than Tamsin's had. Before that Sasha tended to play with the same items at home in a seemingly repetitive manner, and she often played on her own at nursery. When happy and doing her own thing she seemed more independent than our older daughter had been, but most of the time she very much depended on me and needed my full attention. I was never allowed to stand around and chat to other mums after group activities, or stop to chat if I bumped into someone I knew in the street. This is still the case today. In later years Sasha developed a phrase to shout at me in these situations: 'chatting gets us nowhere'. Sasha had no patience and did not seem able to occupy her own mind or thoughts or just observe the world around her in a way that other children would.

Having already been through the toddler stage with our first-born helped me immensely in terms of realizing life was different for our youngest. My heart goes out to those who don't have older siblings for their autistic children as I am sure that makes all these indicators much more difficult to recognize. I also very much appreciate how lucky we were in terms of having the support of our family. Understanding Sasha's behaviour must have been more difficult for them, at least initially, because they did not live locally, so they rarely got to see her over a sustained period of time. It was a great relief that we were listened to, and believed, and I truly wish that this could be the case for every family.

ADVICE FOR PARENTS AND CARERS

- Educating friends and family about your child can help them understand your child's reactions better. This might mean they will be more supportive. The PDA Society has plenty of resources that can help with this.

- For help with understanding the assessment process for an EHCP, the IPSEA and SOSSEN websites and helplines are highly recommended. It is important for parents to know what their child is legally entitled to. It is worth noting, however, that in most cases there is likely to be a fight for this support.

- The EHCP process can feel daunting; there is a lot of paperwork and there are also timescales that should be kept to (but that the Local Authorities often fail to meet). Collecting evidence about your child is part of this process and reports from professionals will help back up your comments about your child. These professionals might include an educational psychologist, speech and language therapist and occupational therapist, but it is also worth approaching anyone outside of your close family who might see your child on a regular basis.

- Many other parents have applied for EHCPs and are happy to share their experiences, but it will help most if you ask for advice from those in your local area.

- Parents and carers can apply for an EHCP directly, the application does not need to be made by a school. Some schools may be overwhelmed with the amount of paperwork they have to manage if they have more than one child with additional needs, whereas parents and carers might be more able to focus on ensuring the information about their own child is correct and sent promptly.

Chapter 4

THE MAINSTREAM SCHOOL YEARS: AGE FIVE TO TEN

After two terms of being in the nursery, Sasha moved up into Reception class at the Infant school. Luckily, because she was a summer-born child, she only had to attend for half days to begin with, and this slow transition helped her to settle. The class teacher and I were given the opportunity to attend an autism-specific training session together and this definitely helped in terms of ensuring we had time to talk about Sasha's individual personality and what kind of support might help her in school.

I think at this point I was still amazed and relieved that Sasha was agreeing to attend school at all, given that I had already experienced how much she wanted to follow her own path when at home. Alarm bells rang though, whenever I was told that there would be no problems, and that Sasha would cope just fine. I already knew how much I was altering my own behaviour to accommodate Sasha and I guessed it would be much harder in a classroom situation. I felt she would need a lot of direct instruction throughout the day, in a specific way, from an individual who understood her, in order for her to be able to cope with the changes that school was going to bring, and to avoid major disruption to the other children in her class.

Early in the Reception year the school asked for volunteers to go into the classroom to listen to children reading out loud from their books. At first I wondered whether it would unnerve Sasha if I did this. I thought she might find it too strange for me to be there with her in school, and that she would want to leave when I left. I need not have worried because she accepted my presence quite happily. I found out that, although Sasha would not read for us at all when she was at home, she was happy to be like her classmates and read to me, or to other parents, when at school. In fact, she read with great expression and intonation, and seemed to have good comprehension. This was just one of several examples of Sasha surprising us over the years!

Initially I was less concerned about how the lessons would go, but thought that some of the other activities during the school day might cause issues. From reading the reports given by nursery staff we had realized that Sasha was not finding it easy to relate to, or play with, other children, so we thought unstructured play times were likely to be difficult. Sasha was already very definite about what she would and would not eat at this stage, so I wasn't overly hopeful about school dinners being a success either, and the school dining hall was a busy, noisy place that I knew Sasha would not like. I also suspected that weekly assemblies involving a lot of sitting down and listening would be challenging for her. While Sasha was in nursery I had been able to regularly attend the school assemblies for our older daughter, and I always enjoyed them. Sometimes when my parents visited us they were able to attend with me – the assemblies brought them great joy too. Tamsin was happy to have me there in the hall for assembly time, preferably on the front row so she could see my face and smile or wave at me. For Sasha's first assembly I reluctantly sat at the back of the hall because I had a feeling that if she saw me, she would want to sit with me. I felt emotional as she walked in with her class, the only child holding hands with an assistant. From a distance I watched Sasha proceed to talk and make noise throughout the assembly, not understanding that she should be keeping quiet and paying attention. It wasn't long before the assistant took her out, realizing it was not a great environment for Sasha. I felt sad for Sasha that everyday occasions which were standard for most other children, including our older daughter, were so difficult for her. There were several assemblies over the three years Sasha attended the Infant school and they were a mixed bag. For some of them, Sasha would leave before the other children did, or she would not even enter the hall at all. There were a handful of special occasions that Sasha did manage to take part in, however. Memories of her standing up to blow out the candles on her school birthday cake, speaking a great line as an angel in the school nativity play and carrying out some planned dance moves with a boy from her class as part of one assembly story being told will all stay with me forever. Nothing was ever as straightforward as it was for the other children though.

Feedback from the Infant school over the three years she was there told us that Sasha did listen to language at an age-appropriate level if a subject was very interesting to her, but at other times she appeared not to listen. I was told Sasha struggled to sit still in a classroom; she would pace around touching objects on shelves or walls. Her eye contact was good for us at home, but said to be fleeting in school. It might have seemed as if she wasn't listening or paying attention but everyone began to realize that she was still taking in information whilst moving around and looking the other way. She had a good level of understanding when it came to topics she was interested in, but her attention levels were inconsistent and dependent on her motivation. It was said that she would flit from one activity to another without concentrating on one task for very long, and one report pointed out that 'the activities that motivate her can vary from one session to the next which can make it difficult to generate a motivating activity as a reward for her'. School said that Sasha did not like using a 'now and next' board but was sometimes happy to use a 'now and next' approach if it was suggested verbally. When Sasha was asked during her second year whether she liked school, she replied with a smiley face emoji. When staff asked what her favourite activities at school were, she replied that she liked play-time, lunchtime and home time the best. I'm sure she wasn't the only child in the class who would have said that though! When pushed for a further response she added that she liked numeracy sometimes, guided reading, PE, ICT (information and communication technology) and music. When asked what activities at school she found hard, she answered, 'All of them. I don't like people being bossy to me', and by this she meant teachers and staff as well as children. I think this was a good insight into her PDA traits. The activities or lessons in school that she told staff she disliked the most were literacy, handwriting, going to the hall for assembly and carpet time. Carpet time was always a problem for two reasons. First, Sasha did not find sitting cross-legged on a slightly scratchy carpet comfortable. She was not afraid to say so and was also not happy with the demand of being told she had to sit there anyway. And second, carpet time generally involved the children sitting still and listening to the teacher, maybe answering questions but without any specific activity to do at the same time. Sasha found it hard to focus and concentrate in this way.

In the summer of her last year at Infant school, Sasha's class teacher called me in to see her. She wanted to let me know that Sasha hadn't been participating in rehearsals for her class summer concert. The concert featured a large amount of singing and dancing, which Sasha actually loved. She just was not a fan of the waiting around, listening to other people, being herded into lines and having to repeat things over and over. So she refused to join rehearsals and played in the classroom at those times instead. The teacher told me, in a caring way, that she thought it was unlikely that Sasha would take part in the concert. She didn't want me to turn up, sit through the whole concert and wonder the whole time where Sasha was.

At the time I found it refreshing that the teacher had thought of my feelings, and had not just battled on, trying to force the inclusion issue. Before that day and over the years to come I would sit through many assemblies, or plays, or masses, or sports days, or other events, watching other people's children. Those children would be participating, sometimes reluctantly, sometimes joyfully, but they were there nearly every time, in the same way that our older daughter was. Sasha was often missing from these group occasions. Or she was there, but didn't take part. Such as in one assembly when the Head asked Sasha's whole year group to stand up and sing the school song. The others all stood and sang beautifully. Sasha remained seated. I often pretended there was something in my eye, as the tears threatened to spill. I felt sad that she wasn't joining in. With hindsight I can look back on those times and see that Sasha was mostly fine and actually happier when not being asked to join in, with one or two exceptions.

After the teacher had spoken to me about the summer concert, but before the actual event, Sasha sang through all the songs that would be in it during a playdate with a friend (playdates did not happen very often, and they always involved my full attention and help to ensure they didn't end in tears). It turned out that even though she hadn't been rehearsing, she still knew the whole show off by heart. It was amazing what she could pick up from a distance even when it did not appear that she was paying attention! Sasha struggled to cope with various aspects of the rehearsing and it led to some very unsettled times. One of the biggest barriers was her wanting things to be exactly how *she* wanted them. For example, the teacher originally rehearsed with them all in a line for one song, which Sasha loved, but when the teacher changed her mind and put them in a square, Sasha could not get past the fact that she had enjoyed it in the line and so she wanted the teacher to change it back. The teacher, meanwhile, was busy trying to direct 120 other children to sing and dance on cue – no mean feat for her. I know some people might assume it would have been better to change back to the line rather than square, but the change was made for a good reason. I understood that on this occasion it would have been tricky to alter the plans to fit Sasha.

Then at the last minute I was informed that Sasha had somehow been convinced to take part. As I took her to school that morning she seemed to be enthusiastic and ready to join in with the concert later that day. I still had my doubts that it would happen. By the time I arrived at school for the show, along with all the other parents, Sasha had indeed changed her mind and was adamant that she was not going to join in. It was agreed that she could sit with me for the performance instead, and we found a spot on the floor at the front where she could see her classmates perform. From the start Sasha was enthralled and the look of delight on her face at watching the others was priceless. She was moving my hands to get me to clap along at relevant points, and she sang all the words of the songs out loud. She would tell me what was coming up next, and when it was the turn of her class to perform their special song, she got very animated. She joined in confidently with all the singing and the actions, from the comfort of my knee. When the song was over, she sighed and said, 'Mummy, I wish I could have joined in.' The school did everything they could to try to include her, but it was a mountain that was just too big for her to climb. From Sasha's side though, it wasn't that she did not want to join in, it was that she could not. Enjoyment and disappointment were mingled together for us both. Sasha found it too difficult to stay for the rest of the assembly, so I took her back to her empty classroom. Once there, Sasha quickly changed out of her costume, back into her school uniform, and then proceeded to treat me to a very special word-perfect solo of the finale song. That brought a lump to my throat. Others probably would not have appreciated what a big achievement it was for her to stay in the hall for the concert, and I don't think they would have understood how much she did actually want to be a part of it.

I can count the number of times Sasha ever agreed to do homework on one hand. It did not matter what I tried in terms of persuading and rewards, there was just no way she would engage unless it was an activity that had excited her for some reason. She seemed to have predetermined that school was where schoolwork should be done, but home was definitely not a place to do work, and there was no convincing her otherwise. For example, I tried all sorts of inventive ways of getting her to learn spellings. I used whiteboards, marked words out with my fingers in sand trays and placed alphabet letters on the fridge, but Sasha rarely engaged and eventually I had to concede defeat. I think the school understood the challenges I was facing at home because they could see the same resistance to academic work at school, and thankfully the notion of Sasha completing homework was put to one side. Sasha still seemed to be doing well in terms of learning and her understanding appeared to be on a par with her peers, but she resolutely refused to write anything down. This meant we had no real proof of her ability. When it came to taking SATs (Standard Assessment Tests) at the end of Year 2, Sasha was not able to sit down and concentrate on them like most of her peers. Instead, she was taken into a quiet room and the staff did their best to elicit responses to the questions. They knew she was able to give good answers, but understood that she was not able to sit and write them down. They tried various ways of helping her, including playing a sound on a music triangle to prompt her to give an answer verbally. We appreciated their attempts; that is the closest Sasha has come to completing any kind of formal testing in education.

I know that Sasha has happy memories of her time at the Infant school. She was in a class where her peers accepted her for who she was and the teaching staff supported her well. We are immensely grateful for the understanding and care extended to her there, by all staff, by her peers and by other parents.

In the autumn of 2011, at the age of seven, it was time for Sasha to make the move to Junior school. Although this Junior school had the same name as the Infant school, it was based in different buildings across the road and they were run as two separate schools. That meant it was the beginning of a new phase and it felt like a big deal. To some extent, every new school year to that point had felt like a fresh start, because Sasha needed time to get used to each new teacher and class assistant. It was just as important for them to get to know all about Sasha, because understanding her challenges and her strengths was key to building a good relationship. This could have been said for every child in the class, but I think the key difference was how vital this understanding was in Sasha's situation, rather than simply a 'nice to know'.

With the help of the local autism advisory service, both Infant and Junior schools worked together on a transition plan for Sasha. A schedule of small events that would take place over her last summer term in Infant school was drawn up. It involved several short visits to the new buildings, including one with me, to show her the different classrooms and playgrounds, and to introduce her to the people in the school. A transition booklet containing photos of the new environment and new staff was made for Sasha. The Junior school staff were invited to a training session about autism, and some visited the Infant school to see how Sasha acted in the classroom there. It was agreed that Sasha would need some extra help in the classroom, but the suggestion was that it should be a 'light touch' and not an assistant who would be next to Sasha all the time. Deciding what support Sasha should have at school was tricky because it was clear that she didn't want to be different, she just wanted to be part of the class. In fact, at this stage Sasha wasn't even aware that she needed any extra help. Plans were put in place for two teaching assistants to share their time supporting Sasha in whatever way she needed.

Over the summer holidays leading up to the start at Junior school Sasha and her classmates were all asked to send a postcard back to their new teacher, presumably so they could talk in class about the different places that had been visited, or activities they had taken part in. Sasha refused to write on the postcard I bought for her but was happy to dictate to me what she wanted me to write on it on her behalf. I made suggestions along the lines of where we had been and what we had done, like making sandcastles on the beach, swimming, going on bouncy trampolines, etc, but Sasha was adamant she did not want any of that on her postcard. She insisted that I write the following: 'Dear Mrs X, I will always be quiet at school, and when you need me to do some work I will try my best.' When I hesitated to write what Sasha was dictating, and instead tried to explain that the aim of the postcard activity was to prompt class discussions, Sasha started to become agitated and extremely upset. So I had to follow her wishes and write exactly what she wanted on the postcard. I never did find out what the teacher thought of her very specific postcard message.

As we approached the new start Sasha had informed us on more than one occasion that she would be good, and behave 'like a big girl' when she started Junior school. Her comment about being quiet led us to believe she had become aware of how important it was to not be noisy. I wish I could have been in the classrooms as an invisible watcher. Was she hyperactive, shouting out, disruptive? Or simply disengaged? Although she would refuse to do work for us at home most of the time, I had seen some signs of completed work from the Infant school. I didn't always find out whether that was work done out of the classroom with teachers individually or whether Sasha had participated in group sessions. I felt I had to trust the teachers to do what was best for Sasha. We didn't feel that being noisy was a particular issue for Sasha at school though; reports had told us that she often withdrew to the back of the class and did her own thing, rather than being loud and disrupting others. Sasha had talked about how it was the other children who did the 'chitter-chattering' and I often wondered if she ever spoke up to tell them off for their noise. A common characteristic of PDAers is said to be a lack of understanding of hierarchy; children often become upset at others not following the rules but not understanding that they are supposed to follow them themselves, and this definitely seemed to apply to our girl.

We had made comments to Sasha about how important it would be for her to do the work at Junior school, because we wanted to prepare her for this next stage. Our overall impression was that at Infant school, she had mostly resisted taking part in activities and rarely produced any recorded work, unless it was a craft session. We thought that her reluctance to write was driven by a fear of not getting it right; it felt like there was some anxiety over the words not being spelt right, and not seeing the words on the page as she imagined them in her head. We had seen one sentence in her handwriting in an Infant school workbook at the start of Year 1, but from what we understood, she had written very little since then. We knew that the amount of formal work would step up at Junior school, and it was clear that Sasha would need some help. Writing was unlikely to just happen of its own accord.

When asked if she was looking forward to the Junior school, Sasha came up with her own word for how she was feeling: 'nervous-cited'. The transition went well initially; Sasha was excited to start at the Junior school and to be closer to her older sister again. As we expected, the first problems were to do with handwriting, but on top of that Sasha found settling down to the demands of school work very difficult. There were several times when Sasha became very upset in the first year at Junior school. The academic work was increasing as we had expected, but despite trying to prepare Sasha for this, it was all too much for her. She only wanted to experience the fun aspects of school, not the serious side of academic work.

Just before Sasha moved to the Junior school the Headteacher who had been there for many years had retired. I was disappointed because I knew she was a kind lady and a brilliant headteacher, and I think she would have ensured Sasha had the support she needed. We had no clue who would come along next, or how life at the Junior school might change. A new headteacher arrived partway through Sasha's first year there. When he did not get in touch with us during the first few weeks I was surprised, because Sasha was one of only two children in the whole school (240 children) who had an EHCP. I assumed that her EHCP would highlight to him that she had considerable learning differences needing attention and support. The first time we met him properly was a few months after he started, at an annual review of the EHCP. This was a formal meeting that included not only us parents and the Headteacher, but also the class teacher, teaching assistants, the autism advisory teacher, a speech and language therapist and an educational psychologist.

The Headteacher opened the meeting and then invited us to talk about Sasha. By this time, I was well used to annual meetings like this so I had prepared a short list of areas where I felt Sasha needed more support at school. There was a focus on social skills; like many parents of children with additional needs, I could see my child struggling to interact with others and I hoped she could have friends, so I asked for something to be done to help her in this respect. Handwriting was an ongoing issue; Sasha would rarely agree to put pen to paper and I wondered if this could be down to difficulty with holding the pen coupled with a lack of practice. Speech and language was another area of discussion because it was clear that Sasha wasn't speaking very much at school. We wanted to explore the idea of Sasha being able to communicate in other ways, such as using technology. I had around five points on my list, none of them earth-shattering, and I wasn't asking for anything ludicrous for Sasha. I remember there being a pause when I finished speaking, then a comment that has stuck in my mind for many years was directed at me: 'This is a *mainstream* school, Mrs Curtis.' In saying this, the inference was that our child should not be at that school because the support she needed was too great. More than that, I was made to feel like we were part of the problem, that we were asking for too much. I am not ashamed to say that I spent the rest of that meeting with tears in my eyes. Attitudes play such a big part in relationships. Sadly, I felt from that point on that we were dealing with someone who did not believe in inclusion, somebody who resented the extra effort our girl needed. This feeling was to be repeated at a later stage in Sasha's education.

Soon after that meeting it was decided that only one of the two teaching assistants who were allocated to Sasha would continue to work with her. That was because, after the first few months there, it had become clear that Sasha enjoyed the relationship with one of the teaching assistants more than the other. That teaching assistant who stayed with Sasha is, I am sure, the reason that Sasha stayed in mainstream school for as long as she did. She had just the right amount of fun, at the same time as finding ways of encouraging Sasha to join in with her classmates or to record some work. Banter is a word that springs to mind; this teaching assistant did not mind Sasha being cheeky, and was not offended if Sasha pushed her away at times.

The teaching assistant would talk with me on a daily basis to feed back to me what was going on in school for Sasha, but also to hear news about what was happening at home for Sasha. That level of communication was key to helping Sasha. She always gave me the impression that she wanted to learn more about how Sasha experienced life, and that included Sasha's time at home. I am extremely grateful to that teaching assistant for all she did to help Sasha. I think in the early years of education, and in fact throughout school at different stages, there can be an underlying attitude that too much involvement from parents is something to be frowned upon. As soon as children start at nursery school they are encouraged to be independent, but for some children, that level of independence remains out of reach, even at a much later age. I appreciate that staff having to speak with, or write notes for, 30 parents of children in their class would take up a huge amount of time, but for some children this kind of communication can make all the difference between success or failure.

After the annual review during that first year of Junior school, the EHCP paperwork drawn up by the Local Authority detailed that Sasha should have 20 hours of support at school, a slight increase from the 15 hours that was noted in her EHCP throughout Infant school. We had always felt the 15 hours didn't reflect her true needs because those hours would not even cover all of the lessons. Break and lunchtimes were unstructured times that Sasha clearly found challenging in various ways, and the schools did not receive funding to support her at those times. Although we were mostly shielded from the financial budget discussions, we do believe that both schools provided more support than the 15 or 20 hours that were officially funded by the Local Authority. We still count ourselves very lucky that Sasha was accepted into such a welcoming and supportive school initially, and we appreciate all the teachers and assistants who supported her.

School life rumbled on and Sasha's attendance level remained high, with only occasional blips. Difficult days were mostly those when something unusual was due to take place, such as special events where the children were invited to dress up, or school trips, sports days or unusual assemblies. The routine weekly assemblies were also difficult for Sasha and along the way various accommodations were made to help, such as Sasha being the first in to the hall, or the last in, the one nearest the door for a speedy exit when she could cope no longer, or being allowed to sit on a chair so that she had a better view of proceedings and could then keep her attention focused for longer. Eventually she stopped attending assemblies at all though, when everyone agreed that they were adding unnecessary stress to her day. The dressing-up days caused problems partly because unusual clothing was a sensory nightmare for Sasha, but also because she found it difficult to recognize others when they were dressed up as different characters. I remember her once telling us that she was scared of the teachers when they were in fancy dress. They weren't in Halloween style outfits, usually just something related to World Book Day or history events, but not being able to recognize them made Sasha feel scared. On the whole she remained positive about school, but after the first two years of Junior school we heard that the teaching assistant Sasha loved would be leaving the school at the end of the summer term. At the beginning of the next school year, it was decided that Sasha should have four different teaching assistants (TAs) during the school week. Even though the TAs were lovely people, the short times she spent with each of them on different days of the week didn't enable them to build up good relationships. There is no doubt in my mind that this played a big part in why Sasha began to struggle.

There were other signs that school was becoming more difficult for Sasha though. Even though it was still only Year 5, the academic workload was increasing in preparation for the Year 6 SATs and Sasha began to tell us more frequently that she didn't want to be at school. Her main difficulties at school were with communication and expressing herself. She still rarely wrote anything by hand and we wondered if that was because she found it hard to hold a pen and physically write. Her attempts at writing would be best described as sporadic, so you can imagine our delight when, out of the blue, she presented us with an amazing eight-page story that she had hand-written as our Christmas present that year. Over the years, Sasha has retained that ability to surprise us!

Towards the end of Year 4, around the age of nine, Sasha had finally become aware of how different she was to her peers. Socializing was a big challenge for her and she couldn't chat with the other girls about typical mainstream topics they liked at that age, such as music, fashion or make-up. School was no longer the fun environment she wanted it to be.

Sasha was unhappy for most of Year 5, which turned out to be her last year in Junior School. I was called to collect her on more than one occasion. School staff told us she was spending more and more time out of the classroom, and she was needing more frequent breaks outside in the playground or on the field during the school day. She would run about, making up imaginative games and releasing energy. During one particularly tough day for Sasha, she locked herself into a toilet cubicle and refused to come back out until I collected her from there. Her mood at home was very subdued and it felt like we were losing our happy, bubbly girl. Then one Monday morning in summer, Sasha stopped short of the main school door and told me, in very few words, that she just couldn't go into school any more. I wasn't surprised. It had been a slow breakdown to this point and I think we all knew it wasn't the right environment for her any more. It was time to try to find her an education better suited to her needs.

The week after she stopped attending, Sasha and I went into

school for a meeting with the Headteacher and the SENCO (Special Educational Needs Coordinator). I had suggested we all meet, in the hope that Sasha could tell them in her own words how she was feeling about school. As parents, we are often accused of putting words into the mouths of our children, or of talking for them. I am aware that words spoken directly by our children carry so much more weight. I suspected Sasha might not say much though, because any conversation is always a struggle for her, but even more so at times of high anxiety. Being back in the school environment that had felt so hard and isolating for her and speaking with the Headteacher was always going to be a difficult situation for her. Questions were asked, Sasha's answers were somewhat stilted and quiet, and then the Headteacher made a comment in relation to what could be done for her at school. 'Anything is possible, Sasha,' he offered with a smile. 'What, like flying when you're pooping?' questioned Sasha, quick as a flash, with a cheeky grin. Tears of amusement sprung out of the corners of my eyes. To be fair, the Headteacher only took a moment to compose himself before responding that aeroplanes have toilets, and the SENCO pointed out that birds do actually poop while flying. One huge positive I have discovered about living with a PDA child is that life is never dull!

We had an emergency review of Sasha's EHCP and during that meeting it was agreed that the mainstream school had tried to support Sasha as much as it could, but it was no longer able to meet Sasha's needs. Sasha was not forced back into school and she slowly began to relax at home, reverting to the happy girl we had known before. We just had to figure out what could happen next for her in terms of education.

ADVICE FOR PARENTS AND CARERS

- A personal one-page profile document about your child can be created at any time, for any situation. I used to update ours for the beginning of every school year and pass it over to any staff who were working closely with Sasha. I suspect some only gave it a passing glance and didn't want to be bothered with it, but the good people would read it and learn from it and adjust the way they communicated with our daughter. There is a post on my blog that gives an example of a personal profile I created for our daughter. If your child is trying any out-of-school activities it might help to email or hand over this information to leaders in advance, to help them feel better prepared.

- Involve your child as much as possible in the school process. Their voice should be welcomed at all stages and can lend weight to what you as a parent are saying. Think about different ways to capture that voice and share it with others; a child could be asked what they do or don't like at school, and their thoughts could be dictated, or written by themselves, or expressed in a picture. A voice recording might help convey both the level of language skills and the underlying anxiety of your child.

- If your child is struggling at school, don't feel you have to keep dragging them in just for a tick in the attendance register. Find out what the issues are and discuss what accommodations could be made to make the environment more suitable for them. Keep in mind that children are unlikely to learn much at all when they are in a state of heightened anxiety.

- Sensory issues can have a big impact on whether a child is receptive to learning. A sensory or fidget box worked well for Sasha. This was a small box containing items which could be used to help with sensory needs, such as stress balls, spinners, blu-tack, small dolls or plush toys. Visual aids, alternative methods of recording work and being encouraged to take frequent sensory breaks are some other good ideas to help with classroom learning.

- Lots of families are willing to share their experiences and ideas of reasonable adjustments in schools which have worked for them. At our Junior school, a small group of children were brought together to cook in the school kitchen during lesson time, and this was used as a different way of teaching skills such as Maths, English and social interaction. Adjustments as students get older might include doing fewer academic subjects, dropping PE or language learning, or using a computer to produce work instead of having to write by hand.

- The demands of the school day can have a knock-on effect on children. Home life might be disrupted due to outbursts caused by a build-up and subsequent overflow of extreme anxiety. School staff might not be aware of this however, so a first step in trying to make improvements could be to share examples of behaviour at home. Keeping the lines of communication open and collaborating with school to find solutions that will help your child is a good idea.

- If your relationship with school is breaking down I recommend documenting the difficulties in writing. Record examples of support that have been offered or tried along with notes as to whether they were successful. I know it is easier said than done, but any email communication with school should ideally be short and not laden with emotion. This may all need to be used as evidence at a later date.

Chapter 5
NOT FINE IN SCHOOL

L ife became more difficult for Sasha as she moved up through the school years and, although there were a couple of happy highlights, the challenges have left a lasting impression. In the months before we reached the point of no return with mainstream schooling, I was very aware that school days were becoming increasingly difficult for her. My feelings were mixed; I felt grateful that Sasha had been able to attend the same primary school as her older sister, relieved that she was able to remain there for as long as she did, and resigned to the knowledge that it was time to move on to a different type of educational provision.

While trying to entertain and educate Sasha once she was out of school, at home all day, I spent time researching local schools, trying to find a more suitable environment for her. When she left the mainstream school, Sasha had been very clear that she did want to go to a school, but that she wanted it to be a school where there were more children like her. In our county there seemed to be a gap in provision for those autistic children who were not able to stay in mainstream settings, but who were not behind in terms of their academic ability. We heard of some specialist schools for autistic children located outside of our county but these would have involved journeys of over an hour in each direction. We knew this would be too much for Sasha to cope with because of her anxiety around transport and travel.

The specialist speech and language provision I had visited before Sasha started Infant school seemed to have a cohort of children who were most similar to how Sasha presented, so we approached them to request a place. We were asked to send her EHCP paperwork and then a short while later we received a letter informing us that the school would not be able to support Sasha's needs. Nobody from the school had met our daughter, so we wondered if their response was because Pathological Demand Avoidance was clearly indicated throughout Sasha's EHCP, and she was being judged as being too difficult to work with – maybe the EHCP did not clearly convey her strengths alongside her difficulties. With hindsight it is easy to acknowledge that the school would not have been suitable for Sasha anyway, but at the time the rejection stung and left us with a conundrum of what to do next.

Other than that setting, the only other schools outside of mainstream fell into the categories of MLD (moderate learning disability) or SLD (severe learning disability). Sasha would not have been classed as having a severe learning need but also did not fall neatly into the MLD category. Everyone involved with her agreed that she was very bright, and that her reading and maths skills were likely to be on a par with her mainstream peers. That was difficult to determine formally though because Sasha had only produced a limited amount of written work. Towards the end of her time at Junior school, a literacy session for parents and children had been arranged. Organized events where children were expected to sit quietly and listen had not been particularly successful over the years, so I was slightly apprehensive about attending with Sasha. I didn't expect to stay very long; I had a feeling Sasha would quickly declare she was bored, and want to leave. I was shocked when, after listening to the Head speak, Sasha unexpectedly wrote some short but insightful answers on the example literacy test paper that the children were asked to complete. Even more surprisingly, Sasha then stuck up her hand and took a microphone from a teacher to give a great answer to a question about the comprehension passage on the paper. Her true ability was being hidden by her regular avoidance of handwriting and by the difficulties she had with complying with everyday demands from other people.

We eventually ended up in a position where we felt there was only one school option to try and that was an MLD school. Sasha fell in love with the setting when she visited. She commented on the wide corridors, touchy-feely sensory displays on the walls, space in the classrooms, big playgrounds and a large sensory room. I had reservations because I didn't know if any of the cohort of children at this school would be anything like Sasha, or whether the staff would understand her, but we had no other options.

Being given a place at any school is not a straightforward process for any child with SEND (Special Educational Needs and Disabilities) though, and it took over eight months of wrangling with the Local Authority for them to give the go-ahead for Sasha to attend this new school. During this time Sasha was at home, watching a lot of YouTube videos and playing computer games. As mentioned earlier, even whilst attending school Sasha had rarely completed any school work at home. We put this down to the fact that Sasha had a very black and white view that school was for work and home was for relaxing. Most attempts at introducing any kind of routine involving school work to our home life had already been rejected by Sasha over the years; she would not accept being taught by me in any kind of formal way.

I assumed professionals and other parents who didn't face the same kinds of daily challenges that we did would judge me for allowing Sasha to have so much screen time, but I also knew it was not laziness on my part, even if others could not see that. I tried to engage her in learning in a number of different ways, but nothing worked for long. I had an old projector and screen at home and on a couple of occasions Sasha agreed that I could research a topic of her choice and then create a PowerPoint presentation for her. The novelty factor won on those days, but it wasn't sustainable, and it became impossible to make her record any kind of work. It had always been like this with Sasha; there was never anything that could be used as a motivation to make her do what we wanted. Although bribes or rewards of chocolate, sweets, toys or books had all worked well for our first-born child, these had no effect at all on Sasha. To an outsider it may have looked like a case of Sasha not wanting to do work, but we knew it was more to do with the fact that Sasha's brain struggled to cope with demands. Trying to impose any kind of consequence for not doing work was pointless as it would lead to extreme, distressed meltdowns that could take hours to pass. Consequences didn't lead to any learning and they didn't teach her any skills to be able to cope with the initial demands.

From a young age Sasha had an iPad, TV or DVD making noise all day long, whether she was watching them or using them as background noise while she did another activity at home. I know some people would like to ask how she managed without them at school in that case, but the answer to that is quite simple: Sasha wanted to be at school. That was her motivation. She was sociable and liked being around other children. She wanted to be one of the crowd, and she desperately wanted to fit in. It was when schoolwork became more serious and pressured, and Sasha was often taken out of the class away from her peers, that school began to lose its appeal. A few years later, Sasha shared how this made her feel when we asked for her thoughts about school: 'I have learnt as I got older, having other people in the room, learning the same things as me, is for some reason really helpful to me, and one-on-ones just make me learning stuff a whole lot worse. I don't know if it's something along the lines of "I'm alone in learning this and that makes me sad" or "the fact I have to be taken out to do this makes me feel alone", but either way, the more the merrier for me.' Sasha asked to go to a school 'with children like me, with autism and other differences'.

While we waited for news about whether she would be given a place at the MLD school, some professionals working with us suggested that I should not make being at home too enjoyable for her. Nobody needed to worry about that though, because Sasha wanted to be in school. The eight months waiting for the new start dragged on for her. One reason for taking her to visit the setting initially was because we knew that we would need her to be on board with the idea of attending. After our visit she had declared it was her 'dream school'. At the start of the Autumn term, after she stopped attending the mainstream school in the Summer term, Sasha was aware her big sister was going back to school but that nothing had been agreed for her. One evening she began to get very upset and I asked if she would like to go back to the mainstream school, wondering if she might regret having decided to stop going there. Her reply was very insightful and reinforced in my mind that she had made the right decision at the right time: 'Yes, I do miss it, but I know I had no friends there. And it's the forcing of work which I just can't cope with.' She carried on with: 'On the outside it might seem ok, but on the inside it's just not good for me.'

Sasha had left her mainstream school in June 2017, but it was April 2018 before the MLD school was ready for Sasha to begin some trial sessions. Members of a Local Authority provision panel had agreed in December that Sasha should have a place at this school, but our SEN Officer let us know that the leadership team at the school had objected to this decision, not believing that the school was a good fit for her. After further discussions the school was persuaded to add Sasha to their roll. Although she was aged ten and officially in Year 6, Sasha began in a small mixed Year 7–9 class with older children because her abilities were at a higher level than the children of a similar age to her in that school. As Sasha's start date approached, I requested a meeting with staff to discuss how they might be able to support her going forward. I was somehow made to feel like a nuisance, as if it was unusual for parents to be granted meetings; the school seemed to assume that because they had Sasha's EHCP paperwork, they would know everything about her. Oh, how I wish it was that simple! During that initial meeting I tried to explain some of the ways that we helped Sasha at home, and the kinds of language we used that did not raise her anxiety. Then I was asked, in a very pointed manner, whether we had any boundaries in place for Sasha. Of course, we had boundaries; Sasha knew right from wrong and she wasn't a child who regularly misbehaved. I was taken aback at the question and the attitude it was asked with, and I instantly knew that it was unlikely that that member of staff would be able to foster a good relationship with Sasha. I worried that this might be a whole-school attitude and I had a big wobble about whether we were doing the right thing by sending Sasha there. But Sasha was excited and looking forward to starting at her new school and I didn't want to pull that away from her.

Thankfully, it didn't seem to be the case that all staff had this attitude. Sasha was thrilled to be starting a new school, with a new uniform, and she was very happy with her new form teacher. I would drive her to school every morning and collect her every afternoon because, although she would have been entitled to transport paid for by the Local Authority, there was no way she would have gone in a taxi with a stranger. School life was good for the first few weeks, but the novelty factor didn't work for long (often known as a honeymoon period, this seems to commonly happen for PDAers). The school had not taken in many pupils like Sasha before and it wasn't long before everything started to unravel. Sasha desperately wanted friends but found it difficult to converse with the other children because they didn't share her specific interests. There were issues around lunchtimes, play times, cooking lessons, assemblies, class trips and more. The school held summer barbecue parties, picnics and a sports day, the kind of events that Sasha had always found difficult in her old school, and then insisted Sasha attend all of these with the other children. Sasha was never comfortable with sitting around chatting with others, without a specific intended outcome. There didn't seem to be much understanding of the fact that Sasha could not cope with all these non-standard social events that the other children mostly seemed to love. Before long Sasha's attendance level began to drop rapidly, because she couldn't face going into school. Around six months after Sasha started, we were informed that she spent a lot of time alone in the class because she hadn't made any friends. We were told that the work level for the other children was well below what Sasha was capable of completing and it was likely Sasha was bored during the day, often choosing to do her own thing at the back of the class. Sasha came home explaining that the other children were 'working on two plus two but I can do a million plus a million'. She wasn't boasting, she was just trying to indicate the different ability levels of those in her class and how she was feeling different to them all. I was upset because Sasha's words confirmed my thoughts that the school was not suitable for her, but there didn't seem to be any other option. Sasha wanted to be around other children, in a typical school setting. She had no desire to be educated at home or out and about in the community; being part of a school was what she wanted.

Around this time Sasha wrote a letter to the Headteacher asking if the school could put on a Halloween event. The school embraced and encouraged her ideas for this event, but sadly, because of social anxiety, Sasha was not able to fully enjoy the occasion or even to view it as an achievement. She moved her attention onto writing (typing) a script for the Christmas show and the school did their best to accommodate her ideas and incorporate some of them, but again the demands of the actual event were too much for her. The show was a joyous occasion for other parents whose children might not otherwise have had a chance to shine, but as I sat watching in the hall, I realized Sasha was the only child from her class to not make it to the stage.

After Christmas, the school team announced they would be making some changes. They were aware of other girls in our county who were having difficulty accessing mainstream schools, so a decision was made to start a trial: a new, small class of girls all with a similar profile to Sasha and all with anxiety around attending school. As parents, we didn't feel particularly involved in any of the process of setting up the new class, it was simply presented to us as a done deal. I didn't argue though, because I knew the situation was not working for Sasha as it was. However, there were only three girls in the new class and I think most parents would appreciate that three is not a good number when it comes to teenage girls. Sasha was the only one of them already attending the school, so the other girls began a slow transition into the school over the spring term. Sasha met with them on different occasions and was super excited after meeting one of the girls because she thought they had lots in common. They seemed to get on well initially, and Sasha was excited about the possibility of finally having a friend in school. When the new class began at the start of the Easter term, there was another short honeymoon period. The school tried hard to manage the relationships and expectations, but for various reasons the class came abruptly to an unsatisfactory ending. The blame cannot be placed on any one person, but I do think that better consideration of all the girls' differing needs might have led to a more positive outcome.

On the other hand, maybe not. This was still a school trying to act like a school after all, and therein lies the problem. Schools and systems are full of demands. For children who struggle every day with a multitude of demands, schools that are trying to make all pupils behave the same are not likely to be the answer.

After the abrupt end, we attempted to find a resolution and a way forward with the school. At this point we found very little flexibility around options for encouraging Sasha back into school. With hindsight, we can now say that maybe that was for the best; the MLD school was not the right setting for her. Desperation at wanting to fulfil Sasha's wish to be in some sort of school environment and the lack of any other options had led us to try that route in the first place, but at best it could be described as a bumpy ride.

No longer attending school meant that Sasha was referred to CAMHS (Child and Adolescent Mental Health Services) and seven months later she was offered an appointment. Sasha was unable to attend, but this did at least prompt some conversations with the Education Support for Medical Absence (ESMA) service in our county. At the beginning of 2020, a member of staff from the MLD school came to our house to visit Sasha for an hour a week, trying to engage her in some learning, but life changed for everyone when the global pandemic took hold and lockdowns began that March. Over the next few months, we continued discussions about how Sasha might be taught by the ESMA service and eventually, in October 2020, it was finally agreed that she could attend some small group sessions with three or four other children. These were to be twice weekly, for two hours each time. Initially, Sasha was delighted to have an opportunity to return to some other environment outside of the home, but over the next few months her attendance began to decline again. ESMA had a focus on producing work in English and Maths, and although the tutors tried to differentiate and make the learning fun for Sasha, she found it increasingly hard to engage, especially when there were frequent changes such as different children at each session and different members of staff.

At the same time as attending these ESMA sessions, Sasha was able to start a trial at a small specialist school. She was excited about the prospect of joining this school because she felt that the type of children who attended it sounded more like her. We had a discussion with the school in February 2021 and it was agreed that Sasha could start trying some Art and Design classes there alongside her ESMA sessions. From March to July of that year, Sasha attended the school for three hours every week and she was happy to be there. She couldn't wait to start attending more often and to feel like she was a part of the school, rather than only there on a trial basis.

The annual review of Sasha's EHCP began in April that year, soon after she had started attending these new sessions. We were taken aback when the Local Authority insisted that the meeting would be held at the MLD school that Sasha last attended almost two years previously, rather than at the new school where sessions appeared to be progressing well. The Special Educational Needs (SEN) Officer from the LA cancelled at the last minute, and nobody from the specialist school attended, but the review meeting went ahead without them. Everyone who attended the meeting agreed that a move to be on roll at this new specialist school would be the best idea for Sasha. However, shortly after that meeting the specialist school called to let me know that Sasha would not be given a place on their roll. The reason given was that they did not believe that Sasha would engage with Maths and English. We knew that these would not be her favourite lessons at school, but Sasha had told us that she was willing to try hard with them and I had already informed the school of this. The school was not willing to let her try joining these lessons though, and instead made an offer that Sasha could carry on with just the three hours per week of art and design 'on a goodwill basis'.

When the final EHCP paperwork arrived on our doorstep nearly three months after the review meeting, the old MLD school was still named in it, meaning Sasha would stay on roll at a school that everyone knew she would not be returning to. We received emails from the SEN team to say that they would try to develop some other bespoke package in addition to the three hours at the specialist school, but it was not clear how that could work. It had been well documented up to this point that Sasha was not able to engage in online lessons, and that she was not happy for tutors to come in to teach her at home. She had repeatedly told us that she was not comfortable with one-to-one lessons because she felt too much pressure from that, and she wanted to be around other children her age. She wanted to be a part of the new school community, and that, coupled with the fact that we didn't believe it was right for her to remain on roll at a school who had no involvement with her, meant that we felt there was no other choice but to make an appeal to the SEND Tribunal about the old school being named instead of the new one.

I will try to keep this section brief; I think I could write a whole extra book about the process of the Tribunal. The SEND Tribunal in England is a legal body that deals with disputes between parents or guardians and Local Authorities regarding SEN provision for children. The process can spread out over many months, and during that period, children are often not receiving suitable education. Mediation needs to be considered before lodging an appeal, then evidence needs to be gathered on both sides before being put before a Tribunal panel consisting of legal and SEN experts.

I feel it is wrong that so many parents end up having to pursue this lengthy, and often expensive, course of action. Too much money is wasted on both sides on legal fees – money that could be better spent on support for the children. The goal for us as parents was to secure the type of education that best suited our daughter's needs, but the Local Authority SEN Officer, despite having never even met our daughter, presumed they knew better than we did about what was best for her.

I spent the summer preparing documents with the help of an advocate, hoping that all the evidence would lead to Sasha being given a formal place at the school she was already happily attending, and that she so desperately wanted to be part of. The school was not happy with our decision to appeal though, and our relationship with them took a sour turn. To be honest, it had already been on tenuous ground from the very first meeting we had there. I had come away from that meeting with the impression that they did not believe in Pathological Demand Avoidance, and that in their opinion it was all about the child choosing what not to do. I still find it quite astounding that an education establishment can be so narrow-minded, especially a specialist environment that should understand that all individuals are unique and have different needs in terms of what learning approaches work for them. They seemed to be closed to learning more, which in my opinion is truly shameful.

The school decided to push for Sasha to have a full timetable in the mornings, mostly made up of lessons they felt that she could cope with. From September Sasha began trying food and gym lessons, which she enjoyed because the teachers were fun and friendly, but these lessons were just Sasha on her own with the teacher, so they didn't help in terms of introducing her to other students. She tried an 'upcycling' lesson but hated both the noise and the smell, and she was then introduced to Personal, Social, Health and Economic (PSHE) sessions. These lessons were to be shared with another pupil, so initially Sasha was excited about that aspect of them. Very quickly though, PSHE stopped working because Sasha realized it was all about 'real life' situations and they were topics she struggled with. She came out one day telling me that she did not want to learn about alcohol, drugs, money and mental health. But she was told she had to attend these lessons and pressure was put on us for her to do so. The rest of the timetable was filled up with lesson repeats, so by the time we reached the October half term, Sasha was expected to go to four hours a week of art, two of gym, two of food, two of design, two of PSHE and three hours of project work. English and Maths were not being offered, but attendance at all the sessions on her timetable was expected and compulsory.

Sasha was predictably both confused and upset with this push for her to do so many sessions, especially when over half of them were going to be just her and a teacher, no other students. By the time our Tribunal date approached at the beginning of November, Sasha was no longer happy to attend the school at all, because it was not providing the environment and interaction that she craved, nor that which we had been told to expect. We had to change our appeal from being a request for a school place to a request for Education Otherwise Than At School (EOTAS), and this meant the Tribunal date was pushed back a month. The Local Authority SEND team was not happy with our request for EOTAS though, and insisted that they believed Sasha should be attending a school. They argued that they had not been given any time to find the right provision. This was exasperating because by this point, Sasha had been out of full-time education for more than two years, with very little effort made by the LA to find a solution. I had been the one who had needed to push for everything that eventually happened during that time. The judge adjourned our case, giving the LA more time to find a suitable school but also to enable us to prepare better details about what kind of EOTAS package we believed would work for Sasha.

A new date was set for early February, which meant I had to try to find evidence for our case over Christmas. I was aware that my opinions as a parent would not be counted as highly as those of a professional, as unfair as that seems. The last time any professionals had been to assess Sasha was in the months after she left the MLD school in 2019, over two years before our first Tribunal date. The LA had sent their own speech and language therapist (SALT), an educational psychologist (EP) and an Autism Advisory team member round to assess Sasha. Sasha was not keen on having strangers in the house asking her questions, and she refused to say anything at all to the SALT. We had already decided to pay privately for an assessment from a well-respected SALT, Libby Hill from Small Talk Speech and Language Therapy. Libby was brilliant at interacting with Sasha, and her report provided some much-needed details about Sasha's abilities and areas of missing skills. A lot had changed since that assessment however, and a third school failing her had affected Sasha badly. She was disheartened and disillusioned and no longer saying she wanted to be in a school. Experienced educational psychologists who will assess children and provide information that parents can present at a Tribunal were all booked up for months in advance, so there was no chance of us being able to engage one, and we just didn't know how to proceed without this kind of backing. Then I stumbled across an amazing organization called Autism Champions. A Specialist Teacher called Dee agreed to come and assess Sasha and write a report for the Tribunal. Dee coming to meet Sasha was our highlight of those difficult couple of years. Like the SALT two years previously, she listened carefully to our thoughts about Sasha before trying to engage, and when she did enter the room to see Sasha, she approached her with exactly the right amount of fun and understanding, not too many questions, and with no ulterior motives other than to find out what was best for Sasha. Her follow-up report was very detailed and captured everything there was to know and understand about Sasha. I am extremely grateful for the help that Dee gave us at a very difficult time. I wish everyone could be as understanding and as dedicated to finding the best solution for the child as she was.

As we approached the Tribunal date I remember writing a document to be used as our opening statement for the judge. It began: 'Sasha is broken right now, and it is school that has broken her. She has attended three different types of school (actually four if we include the medical absence service); she wanted to go to them, she kept turning up despite the fact they were difficult environments for her, but ultimately she was not given the individual, personalized support that she needed. She calls herself weird, and strange, and says that she would kill herself if it wasn't for the fact she knows it would be painful.' Shortly after writing that, we received the statement of evidence from the small specialist school. The school team stated that they felt it was important to distinguish between when a child's needs are stopping them from accessing the work on offer and when it is simply learned, chosen behaviour. The inference was that Sasha was choosing to not engage. They stated that the school had supported huge numbers of pupils who had been disenfranchised with education for most of their lives and who adopted demand avoidance as a strategy to continue to disengage. Sasha did not actually fit the description of their typical cohort, because she very much wanted to be a part of that provision and she was ready to engage. It was clear to me that the school was not prepared to support Sasha. Although individual teachers were much appreciated because they were working well with her, I felt others had not taken the time to understand her. The overall attitude coming through in the Tribunal statement was that we as parents were at fault, it was nothing to do with the school.

Both school and LA seemed to be ignoring all the evidence we provided showing that Sasha's demand avoidance had existed from a young age and was not only related to education specifically. The statement from the school declared that although they understood that Sasha had complex needs, they didn't feel they were 'as considerable as many others who have succeeded in a school environment'. They expressed their opinion that they felt that we as parents 'believe that the PDA type behaviours precludes Sascha [sic] from the childhood others enjoy'.

They added that they felt Sasha's life was devoid of any meaningful challenge and that it wasn't 'representative of real life or the approach that would support her to become a successful adult'.

These words were like a kick in the gut. It was the first time I had felt accused in black and white of not doing what was best for our daughter. During the Tribunal I pointed out the fact that Sasha had been willingly attending that setting for a period of six months. I took Sasha there for every session, three hours a week, and I think a specialist school could be expected to use that time to build relationships and figure out a way forward that could have been successful for Sasha. We certainly weren't stopping them from telling Sasha what to do during the time she was on their premises. Despite all their experience of teaching children with special educational needs, they were unable to provide a suitable education for Sasha, and it seemed unfair to be trying to deflect that blame and their failings onto us.

The LA eventually notified us just a few weeks before our new rescheduled Tribunal date that they were consulting with three new schools out of county that we had never heard of. Although I imagine the schools they were proposing are good for some children, none of them sounded in any way suitable for Sasha, not least because they were all a long distance away. Sasha struggled with any kind of travel even at the best of times, never mind for a daily journey to school, and that fact had been repeated every year in her EHCP paperwork from when she was nine years old. There were many other reasons why we felt these provisions would not work in terms of what they were offering Sasha, but on the day of the Tribunal, one of the schools gave evidence suggesting that they could be flexible and would do whatever Sasha needed. The judge ruled that this school would therefore be suitable and Sasha was put on roll there. It was not the outcome we had hoped for, and as I read the judgement I felt both sick and angry. When my emotional response subsided, I realized that the judge had to make that decision because the law currently only allows access to EOTAS if there is no suitable school. It is difficult to argue against a school being suitable if they say they can and will do anything for your child. At this point I feel it is worth mentioning that, in 2021–2022, SENDIST panels upheld Local Authority decisions in only 3.7 per cent of cases, meaning rulings were given in favour of parents in 96.3 per cent of cases.[1] I believe Sasha's extreme levels of anxiety and avoidance made our situation very difficult to assess. During the Tribunal I was dismayed about some of the inaccurate information about Sasha and our situation that was used as evidence by the LA and schools. After the Tribunal I sent a Subject Access Request (SAR) to the LA and the two most recent schools that Sasha had attended, in an attempt to shine some light on where these inaccuracies had come from. I felt guilty for using up the time of staff in education when asking for these reports, but at the same time I needed to uncover the facts surrounding what had gone wrong for Sasha. Whilst it was interesting to note the kind of conversations and assumptions that go on behind parents' backs, I wouldn't recommend that all parents ask for this kind of information. It is not for the faint-hearted and can make parents feel even more stressed and isolated when they realize that others don't understand their child. One underlying theme I noticed from the records from the last two schools Sasha had attended was the feeling that I was regarded as a parent who bothered others with detail about my daughter. Education staff are busy, and many of them don't have time to read information parents share with them. My main aim was always to ultimately help my child with the comments I provided. I realized that knowing more detail about Sasha and how

---

1   www.specialneedsjungle.com/send-tribunal-2022-3-7-la-success-rate-government-understand-law-matters

different situations affected her would also help the staff to be more likely to have success. What I couldn't do, sadly, was make the relevant people read the information I provided, or make them believe in how much of a difference the approaches we used made, in terms of encouraging successful interactions with Sasha. However, within the SAR paperwork I did also receive confirmation that Sasha was not to blame for the failures and I hope that will help Sasha if she does ever feel ready to talk about this period in her life. Currently, any mention of what happened or even the word school sends her into a depression, so we try to avoid bringing it up unless necessary.

As I write this book, Sasha's education is still very much up in the air, so I am not able to provide a happy ending to her school story, sadly. We are hopeful that the people now involved do understand PDA and that they have listened to us in order to understand Sasha, but they are still part of a system that isn't always as flexible as it needs to be. Lots of the typical solutions for children who cannot cope with school are simply not suitable for Sasha. Equine or other forms of animal therapy is often suggested for children who struggle with formal school settings, but Sasha is not interested in or comfortable with most animals. Tuition at home doesn't work for reasons already covered and outdoor activities or forest school type activities present a few challenges, including but not limited to Sasha's anxiety about bad weather. Sasha has developed her own skills in digital art and video creation and we hope these can be encouraged and enhanced. Traditional academic subjects hold no interest for her.

At the point at which Sasha was no longer able to attend her mainstream school, we were treated with compassion and understanding. We were not chased by an attendance officer, or threatened with fines, unlike many families in this country. Some might suggest this was because the mainstream school were happy to not have her there any more; any child with additional needs who needs the level of support Sasha did is definitely a pressure on both resources and budget. But we were never made to feel as if that was the case; at an emergency review meeting in the weeks after Sasha had said 'no more', everyone agreed that the school had provided all the support it could but the environment and learning style was not suitable for Sasha once she reached that stage. While I did reflect and wonder whether having one dedicated teaching assistant for Year 5 rather than four different ones might have helped Sasha stay in that school a little longer, it was clear that even if she had made it to the end of Year 6, there was no way she would cope in a large mainstream secondary school.

Being chased and hassled to try to force Sasha into school would have been a huge extra stress on us all at an already difficult time. I was grateful to the mainstream school for showing an understanding of the situation and relieved we were not being threatened with fines for non-attendance. I see lots of stories online from other families of children who are not fine in school because the child's needs are not being met, and in many cases it appears that the schools have high attendance targets to reach so they feel the need to pass that pressure onto parents. In fact, we were to experience this ourselves with the schools Sasha went on to attend. I was surprised to learn from the MLD school that they are held accountable for the same high attendance percentages as mainstream schools, which feels wrong when lots of children with SEND have very specific needs that may be more difficult to meet in a school setting.

The term 'Not Fine in School' has stemmed from the experience of many parents who have struggled to get their children to school, only to be told that their children are 'fine' once they are in school. Parents are often made to feel that the distress they see their child experiencing is somehow caused by the parents. The inference is that if the child is fine once in school, the problem must lie at home. Many autistic girls, and some boys, tend to mask their difficulties in school and I have heard from many parents who say this is true of their PDA children. In Sasha's case, we always felt that her behaviour was observed to be very similar in school to how she acted at home, and maybe that helped us to be believed, at least initially. Sasha was mostly fine in school, with support, until she wasn't. There is a large online community of parents and carers who have children who are not fine in school, and I frequently recommend it to others. During the times when Sasha was no longer able to attend school, we felt well supported with advice and examples of real lived experience from other families in this community.

School Refusal is an expression frequently used but recently there has been much discussion around this term. It seems to imply that the child is making a simple choice about going to school. Although it is true that Sasha reached a point where she refused to enter the mainstream school, there were reasons for this and it wasn't because she didn't *want* to go to school. In fact, Sasha made it clear that she did still want to go to school, but that she felt she needed to be in a school with more children like her. Some Local Authorities have switched to using the term Emotionally Based School Avoidance or similar rather than School Refusal, but, again, this suggests that the problem lies with the child. Many parents now prefer to use the term School Attendance Barriers, because this highlights that there are many reasons why some children are not able to attend school – the environment, the lack of SEND support, anxiety, illness and more. Often reasonable adjustments can be made for children, so that they are supported to attend. However, I believe that the school system is not the right environment for a number of children and the current rules make it not possible for enough adjustments to be made to accommodate all individual needs in many settings. I believe there are cases where schools could be more flexible and understanding though, and all avenues should be explored in this regard.

Every time Sasha made it clear that the environment was not suitable any more, I did not force her to go to school. I have heard stories from other parents who have been told to drag their children into school or for their children to try touching school gates as a first step to resolving anxiety about being in school. Sasha was already nearly as tall as me at the age when she stopped mainstream. There was no way I would have been able to physically drag or force her to go anywhere. All our evidence from home and from staff in previous school years had shown that if Sasha was not happy or comfortable doing something, there was no way to make her. I knew that legally she did not have to be in a school, she just needed to receive an education suitable to her age, ability and aptitude, considering any special educational needs she had. Holding the Local Authority to account to provide this suitable education for our daughter has turned out to be impossible.

The impact on a child's mental health from being in the wrong setting should not be underestimated. Sasha very much feels like she is the broken one and that she is the one who has failed. Of course, we know, and have tried to tell her, that the truth is that she has been failed. By the system, and by certain people within it.

I know there are some brilliant people working in education who are prepared to stand up and fight the system in order to achieve what is right for the child and family. We desperately need more people to understand that education cannot be a one-size-fits-all kind of box. For some children, the current offerings in terms of provision will never suit them. Ignoring that fact is breaking families and creating huge mental health issues for the children.

ADVICE FOR PARENTS AND CARERS

- Protecting mental health has always been a key factor in decisions I have made for our daughter and I urge others to do the same. Some people may judge this style of parenting as weak, but I have felt strong about doing what is right for my child. I recommend not putting the system first, and not worrying about what others think of you.

- I have been asked many times how to know when enough is enough when it comes to school attendance. I wish I had a simple answer, but the truth is nobody has a crystal ball and it varies from child to child. Whilst I would like to say that we made the call to change schools at the right time, it is difficult to know whether a decision made earlier would have been better. All we could do was gently encourage our daughter to go but then listen to her when she said it was enough.

- Remember that the school system has a curriculum and targets set by our government. Try not to take things said or done by staff too personally. It is true that attitudes really matter though, and finding a school with open-minded people who are prepared to listen to what helps your child can make all the difference.

- Every child is different; for some children home education or working with tutors in or out of the home might be a better option. School is a challenging environment with many demands and it can often be difficult for a PDA child to manage. Think about what could work for your child and do not be afraid to challenge the system.

- Please do not feel alone if you are having struggles with getting your child to school; there are many families who go through the same and who have good advice to share.

- For any parents of children who are experiencing difficult times at school, I wholeheartedly recommend the Not Fine in School website and Facebook group for lots of support and information (www.notfineinschool.co.uk).

- Another great source of information that I have learnt much from over the years is the Special Needs Jungle website (www.specialneedsjungle.com). This not-for-profit organization provides detailed information for parents and carers of children and young people with special needs and disabilities.

Chapter 6

ANXIETY AND MENTAL HEALTH

There are many aspects of everyday life that we felt Sasha experienced differently from her older sister. I have grouped these into some common themes below.

Leaving the house

Leaving the house with Sasha was never straightforward or easy. Pathological Demand Avoidance means that she is living with an extremely high level of anxiety. This affects her in all sorts of ways, but the biggest impact is on what she is able to do. It is not only demands that others might try to place on her which are a problem, but also demands which she places on herself, and this is more evident when we think about activities that others would consider to be fun and enjoyable. Typical everyday activities are full of demands and sensory challenges, from getting dressed in the morning and brushing teeth, to travelling to school and attempting any sort of academic work. But something that many people take for granted, leaving the house to do a fun activity, can still be seen as a demand and will often bring on avoidance. Taking Sasha out for a fun activity was rarely easy, even when she was younger.

Lots of other children, including our older daughter, will do all of the usual everyday activities asked of them, even if they are not always happy about it. When it comes to doing something fun, they are more often than not excited and said to 'jump at the chance'. It is, and always has been, different for Sasha. Some of the following examples might help explain just how much is involved in leaving the house.

These days, any time we make it outside and Sasha breathes fresh air, I rejoice silently. Those times are few and far between. Despite her constant avoidance, I am always trying to think ahead and come up with new ways to engage Sasha, different suggestions of what we could do, in the hope of enriching her life. We do very little on a daily basis at the moment, but my photos amassed over the years since the girls were born show many days out and activities that we tried along the way. Those occasions were not always successful, but we tried our best and we had many fun times.

During the years when Sasha was at nursery and primary school, I preferred to spend more time at our house rather than visit others, because it was less stressful for me when Sasha was in an environment she was comfortable with. I would invite friends over to our house for coffee or lunch, not because I had an innate desire to always be the host, but simply because it was easier for me to feel relaxed and enjoy the company of others when I knew I didn't have to be on high alert. It wasn't because I didn't want to visit their beautiful houses (which I always felt would be less messy than ours), or because I didn't want to make the effort to go out. Sasha was comfortable in our house and was able to escape to her own quiet space. If we stayed home I didn't have to deal with her getting upset/ overwhelmed and demanding to go home every few minutes, and I didn't have to worry that she was going to make a mess or pick the paint off someone else's wall (this actually happened once!). I hoped that my friends understood that I would have loved to visit their houses, or to be joining in with picnics, playing in the park, attending festivals, going to the zoo or any other group activities, but it was just too difficult. Occasionally I would say no to invitations to join in the fun elsewhere because I didn't like the idea of being flaky – I knew there was a high chance of turning up somewhere but then having to leave ten minutes later due to a meltdown. Sometimes I would say yes because I was desperate to try and enjoy a day out just like other families would be doing, and I wanted that for our older daughter too. Other times I had to be non-committal and last minute with deciding what to do, which was very difficult for someone like me who loves being organized and having a plan.

Going out to have fun experiences did not get any easier as Sasha got older. Towards the end of the second year in Junior school, Sasha became more aware that she was different to her peers. She didn't want to be different though, she wanted to be the same as her classmates. So, when a school trip to see Aladdin at the theatre in London was announced, Sasha insisted that she wanted to try to go along with the class. Transport was to be via a coach journey that would take at least an hour each way. We already knew that Sasha found all kinds of travel difficult, so I wasn't at all sure she would cope with the coach journey. I offered to take her separately by car or by train instead, as I thought that allowing her to be in a quieter environment would reduce some of the sensory impact. Sasha was adamant that she wanted to stay with the others and try the coach though. I made the decision to travel with her because I knew that an exit plan would be needed if the whole excursion became too much for Sasha to cope with. The school support staff were already stretched with looking after a big group of children, and I didn't want any of them to have to miss out on the show if Sasha needed to leave. The coach journey there was just about manageable for Sasha because we made sure she was sitting at the front where she could see the road, further away from the children who were making lots of excited noise with their friends. We arrived at the theatre and Sasha was already feeling a bit wobbly, then within five minutes of the theatre lights going down and the show starting, Sasha was already asking in a loud voice to leave. That was just one of many activities we have tried but have had to leave early from over the years. The money aspect has been slightly irritating at times, in terms of having to pay a lot for activities that were not able to be enjoyed, but I would have happily paid more if I could have ensured she would enjoy the experience. The day of the theatre trip I was simply relieved that I was there with her and able to take her home by train. The alternative would have been a much bigger meltdown if she had been forced to stay. We had experienced something similar a couple of years before when we had booked a family outing to see Disney on Ice. Despite having front row seats, Sasha found the whole event too much of a sensory overload and I had to leave the arena with her. She and I spent the rest of the show sitting in the entrance area, waiting for the end of the show. We were not able to go home at that point because her dad and sister were still in there enjoying it – luckily I was well prepared and had taken some technology along to entertain her while we were waiting outside!

During the period when Sasha first stopped being able to attend the MLD school, while we were trying to find a better option for schooling, I tried to create opportunities for less formal learning. We heard of lots of great sessions for families who were home educating their children, but it was difficult for Sasha to leave the house and join them. She never did anything without a good reason or a desire to go somewhere, and even if she did want to go out, there were many factors and situations that would cause her huge anxiety. I had to spend a lot of time gently encouraging her to think of anything she might like to do, and then I would have to put a lot of effort into preparing for these mini outings. I was all too aware of how quickly an excursion could go wrong, even with extensive planning. We tried some trampolining sessions for home educated children; Sasha loved the bouncing, but the time off the trampoline, waiting her turn, was extremely difficult. She wanted to interact with the other children attending the sessions, but didn't know how to speak to them or how to join in their games. It brought home to me how amazing it is that so many children assume roles when playing, without any written rules or instructions; many can flex to follow the lead of others, or are socially aware enough to know how to gain that control for themselves, or can figure out how to create an even balance in a group. Sasha could do none of those things, she simply didn't have the same skills as her peers and wasn't able to acquire them, no matter how we tried to teach her.

Sasha had a burst of nostalgic feelings around this time, so we attempted to recreate some happy memories. Nothing was ever straightforward though. I remember heading to an old playground we used to frequent when the girls were younger, only to find it was full of preschoolers when we got there. Happy about the idea of the playground only minutes before when we left our house, Sasha then became rooted to the car seat when we arrived at the playground and saw the young children, saying she was too old for it and that she would only be happy if there were other children her age there. I had to gently explain to her that most of the other children her age were in school. I knew from previous experiences that going after school or at weekends would mean the playground would be too busy and overwhelming for Sasha. She was unable to get out of the car that day and has not returned to any playground since. This is another challenge we have faced repeatedly; disappointments last a long time, and if something, somewhere or someone goes wrong, Sasha is unlikely to be able to try the same thing again in the future.

On a different day, Sasha asked if we could revisit Paultons Park, a theme park that she had enjoyed when she was younger. I was uneasy about this idea because I knew that Sasha had only gone on the Peppa Pig themed rides previously, but by now she was 12 and much taller than the toddlers who were generally found in this area. However, I was keen to encourage any time out of the house and did not want to put her off. The trip nearly didn't happen because when she realized it would be a long journey, Sasha was almost too anxious to get in the car. When we finally made it there, we went to the office to ask for their Queue Assist pass again, as we had when she was younger. This was an accommodation we found necessary to request because we knew that being in queues and having to wait increased Sasha's anxiety, and that would more often than not lead to a meltdown. Not a small upset that could be recovered from quickly, with distraction such as a food treat or a different activity, but a full-on meltdown that would mean the day was ruined and we would have to leave for home. On this visit, because of her height, the difference in age between Sasha and other younger children waiting for these rides was very obvious. That led to a lot of wobbles on Sasha's part. The day was full of stress because Sasha kept questioning whether it was right for her to be there, but her nostalgic desire to ride the Peppa Pig rides again won out in the end, and they did give her great joy. It wouldn't have been obvious to others that she was constantly fighting those battles with her own mind. I am sure that day we received a lot of 'looks' and judgement for what some see as queue-jumping, but what we know to be the only way we can access rides that many other children can easily wait for.

Another time I suggested visiting a shopping centre just for somewhere to go and something to do, a change from being at home so much. I hoped that exposing Sasha to a different environment might help acclimatize her to life outside the house in some way. In the middle of the shopping centre, we came across a giant chess set and a table tennis table, and Sasha enjoyed playing with both for a short while. We hadn't known they would be there, so that was an added bonus to our trip, and the fact the centre was quiet because it was a school day definitely helped too. For a girl who would rarely leave the house, each one of these excursions was a huge achievement and I used any small opportunity I could as a chance for her to learn. We looked at price tags and did some basic maths, read any wording on signs, learned how to read a map and so many other ways of gaining new skills. I wasn't sure if we were attempting home educating, de-schooling or unschooling at this point. All of these forms of learning have merit in my view, but for our girl who struggled to leave the house or to engage in many activities other than those of her own choosing, none seemed like the perfect way forward for us. In Sasha's mind, she was still keen on being a part of a school, which is why we felt we had no choice but to pursue that option.

In the autumn I took Sasha ice-skating, one of the few activities that she has enjoyed over the years. That doesn't mean she has always been able to go skating even when she has wanted to though; there have been times when the demand avoidance has prevented us from even leaving the house in the first place. Then there are the times when her anxiety over a variety of issues has taken over, such as how many people would be there, or the type of skate boots she would get to hire, or whether she should wear a coat or not. I wrote about our skating trip on my blog and an anonymous commenter implied that we were wrong to be doing fun activities rather than making our child go to school. 'You shouldn't have taken her skating during the day. You are just pandering to her. She is not at school, so she should not be out having fun. You should be making her work at home during the time other children are in school.' I felt attacked, and this comment gnawed away at me for a few weeks. Rather than question myself about whether I was right to take Sasha to do these activities though, instead I wondered whether I should stop sharing details of our trips out online. Those times we made it out of the house to do anything at all were more than simply 'fun'. They were small victories, intended to help prevent Sasha's mental health from declining. I realized that the person commenting had no idea at all about our daily lives and the amount of effort that was going into making any trip outside of the house, and I decided to push that comment to the back of my mind.

I think, with their comment, this person was trying to tell me that if I kept Sasha in all day for the hours other children are at school and didn't let her do fun things, Sasha would somehow eventually give in and be able to return to and cope with school. I liken this situation to those people who suggest that the way to deal with fussy eaters is by putting only the food you want to give them on the plate. Nothing else is allowed; eventually, when they are hungry enough, they will eat what you want them to. We tried this with both our girls when they were younger. It worked for our eldest, but not so with our youngest. We had experience of trying the usual parenting options first, and if typical methods had worked, we would have stuck to them. Life would be a lot easier!

Any simple trip out of our house still involves a huge amount of forward thinking and planning. Getting Sasha in the right mood where she feels able to leave is not a simple task. The planning generally starts some time in advance, talking her through it, providing options, always having a plan B, C and sometimes even Z. Occasionally though, telling Sasha the plan at the last minute proves to be a better strategy, so she doesn't have time to worry or get too confused about what is coming up. It is a constant guessing game as to which of those strategies (advance warning or last minute) is best. Using the right language and never giving the impression of rushing is key to making it out anywhere. Even if we are going to be late, there needs to be a smile on my face and an 'oh well, it doesn't matter' attitude. Time is an extra pressure that will raise anxiety levels even more. It is important that my body language and tone of voice do not reflect any of that pressure because Sasha is extremely quick to pick up on emotions and add them to her own.

Sasha has always struggled with travelling anywhere, on any mode of transport. She has always worried about leaving items behind on public transport, and she has always felt travel sick. There has only been one occasion when she was physically sick, but her anxiety over feeling ill and the slim chance that she might be sick is always forefront in her mind. Sasha will not take any medicine at all, so instead she uses anti motion sickness wristbands, even for short journeys, and we have to travel with the car windows down whatever the weather. Those solutions do not seem to make much of a difference however, and her anxiety is still sky high. As already mentioned, having to cope with the demand of leaving the house is an extra challenge, even when it is for something she really wants to do. On top of the difficulty with travelling is the additional anxiety about what is coming up in terms of situations and people who will be there – potentially having to interact socially when we do finally reach a destination.

There is a phrase I often repeat when trying to explain our life with Sasha: 'It's the little things.' The little things matter. One recent example of this was when our neighbour asked me if I would mind taking their dog for a walk around lunchtime on a day later in the week. I happily agreed to help; I love dogs, I love walking and I knew I would need a break from my desk where I am often busy writing. That day I mentioned to Sasha in passing that I had been given this important task to do, but I knew not to have too big a conversation about it or to ask her if she wanted to come with me because the answer would have most definitely been 'no'. Then on the morning of the walk I reminded her that I would be walking the dog at lunchtime, and I threw in a 'You could come too if you like'. When I took lunch to her a couple of hours later I commented on how the weather was perfect for dog walking – not too hot, not too cold, not too windy, not too wet. Weather is important to Sasha. She agreed, and told me she would maybe come with me. I replied great, then left her to eat. Five minutes before I was thinking of leaving the house, I said, 'Shall we go then?', and by this point Sasha had started to waver. So, then I spent ten minutes trying to joke her into getting up from the sofa and leaving the house. I am sure a similar situation involving difficulty leaving the sofa might occur in many households where teenagers reside, but the difference with Sasha is that it is not simply about how comfortable the sofa is. We always have to make this much effort for any trip out of the house, from planning the details to getting the communication just right. This is how we have had to approach pretty much every situation ever since Sasha was born. That day I quietly rejoiced on the inside when Sasha finally agreed to come, knowing that I had to show very little emotion so as not to throw her off course. She only has one set of clothes that she is currently happy to wear, so I went upstairs to grab them for her, knowing that it would be too much effort for her to go and get the clothes herself. If I had insisted on her going up to dress herself, or even suggested it, our excursion would be called off.

We headed off to the neighbour's house, but Sasha would not come in with me to collect the dog, preferring to stand outside on the drive at a safe distance. At different times over the years, she has said she likes dogs, but she becomes more anxious when they are excited or if they bark. Unpredictable behaviour is difficult to cope with, and this shows when she is around younger children too. Sasha wore her headphones so she could listen to music as she walked and we headed off towards a local park area. Sasha walked ahead but the dog was a little slow, and it wasn't long before Sasha was a long way in front, seemingly oblivious to the fact she was no longer walking with us. Eventually she did stop to check where we were, and she seemed slightly irritated by the fact that the dog and I were unable to keep up with her. This pattern of her being ahead, stopping and barely waiting for us to catch up before she continued walking carried on until we reached a narrow alleyway. I instantly regretted my decision to suggest we head in this direction because there were lots of flies around there and I was on edge, waiting for Sasha to say she wanted to return home because she couldn't bear them (insects are one aspect of being outside that she dislikes). Amazingly, she carried on walking; I am sure it was the distraction of being able to listen and sing along to her own music that helped her get through the flies. After some time out of the house we did reach a point where Sasha was walking next to me rather than some way in front, but when I tried to talk to her she would point to her headphones and say 'I can't hear' rather than engage in any conversation. The only time she took them off was when we reached an open green area with a playground, an area she had never been to before. As we sat on the swings Sasha began to chat animatedly about what a perfect place it would be for a picnic with friends, saying how much she wished she could do that, but then eventually talking herself back out of it with the knowledge that she doesn't enjoy being outside, relaxing, with no fixed aim, having to cope with flies and other people, and the fact that she doesn't have any friends to share this with anyway. As a parent, it is heart-breaking to know that your child wants, but is unable to do, such simple things which come so easily to many of their peers.

It was a warm day, and as we headed home I was glowing inside with the knowledge that Sasha had stuck it out and completed a fairly long walk with me. The dog's owner lives a couple of doors past our house, so as we approached our front door I offered Sasha the key to our house so that she could get home more quickly. She refused though, unable to complete this seemingly small act of independence, choosing instead to come and stand outside the neighbour's house again as I took the dog back in. It suddenly struck me that the majority of Sasha's peers, around the age of 15, would be able to make simple or even much longer trips out of the home independently. Sasha is always with me, unable to face the challenges and demands of life outside the house.

When we got back into our house after the dog walk, I offered Sasha an ice lolly as it was such a hot day. I was already fairly sure she wouldn't accept one because she only ever drinks water and she eats the same few food items every single day. I still offer though. Her response as to why she didn't want a lolly was 'No, because that has taste', which made me laugh.

As I write this, Sasha has left the house just 19 times in the last nine months. Her experiences with the previous education settings definitely had an impact on her ability to leave the house; the lockdown events of 2020–2021 didn't help but they were not the beginning of this downward trend in getting out. At the start of the year, at Sasha's request, we made a few trips out to go ice-skating again, and we visited a McDonalds to see if she could face sitting down to eat in the restaurant (although she loves their fries, she prefers to eat them at home, in peace). We went to Hobbycraft once, a place she used to love, but she has now decided she doesn't want to buy anything from there and will not go again because making things takes too much effort. Reading between the lines, I can tell that it is the perceived demand or pressure of having to do something with any items bought. I definitely do not put any demand on her with regards to this, but her own internal thoughts create the demand.

Other times we have left the house this year have included an optician's appointment, a surprising agreement to visit a maze at a National Trust property (mainly because she wanted to see if she could cope with the feelings of being in the car for a slightly longer journey), one dog walk as mentioned already and one other walk around a park. Walking is not something Sasha usually agrees to do; there has to be a purpose to a trip out and walking is not something she considers fun. The weather conditions were just right for her that day; not too warm or cool, a little bit windy (although probably not windy enough for her liking, she loves to see leaves swirl) and there was a lovely blue sky with white clouds. We also picked to go at the time of day she prefers, later on as the sun was beginning to set. Sasha only agreed to walk because it was an opportunity for her to listen to her music playlist – she won't often do that in the house because YouTube tops her favourite activity list. When out, she walks with headphones on, listening to her music and totally ignoring me and any comments I might make about the scenery or other people.

We were also able to spend a weekend at CenterParcs. This has been the only holiday destination we have consistently enjoyed with Sasha over the years. We have now reached a stage where Sasha cannot travel anywhere else for a holiday. The familiarity of the CenterParcs lodges and surroundings, coupled with the Subtropical Swimming Paradise which means swimming every day is possible, are a big enough pull for Sasha to overcome the anxiety induced by the travel to reach the destination. That doesn't mean it is an easy trip though; we still have to do lots of preparation. We are never quite sure if Sasha will be able to leave the house to travel there in the first instance, Sasha is not able to make use of most of the activities on offer and there is always a variety of issues during the time away. We always follow the same pattern of daily timings for each day of our break. Nothing is plain sailing; Sasha can't choose to switch off her anxiety for something that would appear to be fun for many others.

I hold onto the hope that we can make some more trips out of the house in the near future – ice-skating again, and going to see the local pantomime. Panto is a family tradition. There are no other shows Sasha would agree to go to because she insists that she doesn't like watching real people. We have managed panto over the years because we started going with other families from school when the girls were young. Sasha loves the slapstick humour, and the show is repetitive so she knows what to expect. We have learnt to only book seats that are on an aisle for easy access in and out because over the years Sasha has often found it necessary to leave early, mid-show. On occasion there were parts of the show that Sasha found unbearable – loud noises, or actors running through the audience with water guns for example – and they also prompted a quick exit. As I write this I am realizing that I book the aisle seat not really for Sasha's sake but for the other families around where we sit. I don't think Sasha has ever worried about disturbing other people, but I do! Being quiet during a show is one of society's expectations that Sasha finds it hard to comply with.

Every trip out of the house has involved a huge amount of preparation and paying attention to the little things. Every trip has brought on extreme anxiety, so much so that we nearly haven't made it out of the door. Every single time. It is exhausting for me, but I imagine it is even more exhausting for Sasha. She wants to go, but her brain makes it difficult for her. As her parent, I feel all I can do is try to get the little things right, then gently encourage and hope that she feels able to make it out. There is no point in trying to force her to leave the house; if her mood is not close to calm and stable before going through the door, it is not likely to miraculously improve when we are out.

Sleep

Bedtime can be a challenging time for many parents of autistic children, and that can be due to difficulties around getting to sleep or the challenge of staying asleep (or both). For some reason, Sasha seemed to decide years ago that going to sleep after midnight would be a bad thing, so although her bedtime was later than others her age when she was younger, at least we knew she would not be up all night. We are not sure if she always slept all through the night but she rarely disturbed us, possibly because she was scared to be out of bed on her own at night time. She would always wake up very early though, and for several years 5am was a regular waking time. Eventually she began to wake a little later, but even now, at 15, when most teenagers would like to spend as much time in bed as possible, Sasha still wakes early. Her body clock is clearly different to that of a typical teenager, and she generally needs less sleep than most. I have heard of some PDA individuals having unusual sleep patterns, and often this is to do with the fact that going to bed and getting your body to shut down and then go to sleep is a demand in itself.

For us, the bigger challenges arose around getting to sleep in the first place. Although it did not appear to be so much of an issue when Sasha was younger, there was definitely a time when her anxieties started to take over. We needed to follow a prolonged routine before I was allowed to leave the bedroom. She seemed to develop obsessive tendencies over issues such as her pyjamas laying exactly flat on her body, and having her cuddly toys in *exactly* the right position. Actions would need to be completed in a certain order and there would be repetition of certain phrases. It could take up to half an hour or more of her trying to lie down before promptly sitting back up and trying to readjust everything over and over again. She also talked about how her mind was too full of everything to be able to get to sleep. She tried hard, but some nights she found herself unable to drop off to sleep, and the only thing that helped was me getting into bed with her. She knew that was not an ideal solution; she didn't want me to have to do that for her, but she could feel that it calmed her down, so we agreed that was what would happen when it was necessary.

For a long while, between the ages of eight and 12, I was having to spend up to an hour sitting next to Sasha in her room, holding her hand to help her feel safe, waiting for her to drop off to sleep. Then I would quietly tiptoe out once she was asleep. I thought this would go on forever but we were eventually able to make a small change, which meant that I could leave the room while Sasha was still awake and then return later to check if she had gone to sleep. This worked for a while, but after a few months we reached a stage where I would leave, but when I returned to check on her 30 minutes later she was still awake. The solution at that time was that I ended up sleeping on a mattress on her floor.

For nearly a whole year when Sasha was 13, I had to sleep in the same room as her in order for her to feel safe. After that we moved on to a stage where Sasha would video call me from her bed while I sat in my own bedroom, so that we were at least 'connected' while she fell asleep. I think there is an unspoken expectation from society that parents must sleep in their own beds, in their own room. I always understood how valuable sleep was, because even though Sasha did not seem to need that much of it, I saw the impact on our daytimes if she did not get enough sleep. So I was prepared to do what it took to make sure we all slept, wherever that was.

Busy, active minds find it extremely difficult to switch off. Too many anxious thoughts about 'what if?' come to the fore when it is all quiet and there is no other activity taking place. I know that some families struggle with children who don't want to go to bed or to sleep because they are having too much fun being awake, or because the demand to go to bed is one they feel they need to avoid, but that did not seem to be the case for Sasha. Trying to pinpoint 'why' sleep is not happening is a good place to start – is it too hot, too cold, are they too uncomfortable, scared of little sounds, scared of the dark? Or is it thoughts of something which has happened at some point in the past being repeated, or fear of what is due to happen at some point in the future, or the fear of not knowing what might happen? We probably started out with a fixed idea of when bedtime should be, as most parents do, but we quickly moved on from trying to enforce this ideal because we could see that was an extra pressure on top of the other difficulties Sasha was facing. If sleep is an area that your family finds challenging, it is definitely worth exploring some of the many resources there are to help find solutions.

Special occasions

There seems to be an unspoken expectation from society that special days should be happy times. They are full of so many challenges though; birthdays, holidays, Christmas and any other kind of special occasions all bring extra demands on top of what is usually expected on a typical day. For many families there are traditions that lead to things being done differently. Sasha always struggled more on these special days. When it was Tamsin's birthday, Sasha would want to open her older sister's presents and would get upset if we tried to stop her. Initially we might have thought of this as a need for attention, but we came to realize it had more to do with anxiety about the unknown and not liking surprises. Sasha could not (and still can't) sign her name on a birthday card for any family members; one reason for this was her struggle with handwriting, but the fact that it was something expected of her also played a part in her avoidance. It made what many of us would consider a simple task feel impossible.

Christmas can be particularly difficult for many; the assumption that everyone should be happy is a demand in itself. Then there is an expectation that people should spend lots of time with family and friends and break from routines. Everyone is expected to cope with the suspense and excitement during the build up to the big day. Panto, a visit to Santa in his Grotto, ice-skating, carol singing, decorating houses, flashing lights, church services, more candles, Christmas jumper day, Christmas parties, school plays, gift buying, not knowing what presents to ask for, gift wrapping, snow (or more likely where we live, disappointment at no snow)... these are just a few of the things which are different and additional at this time of year, and which may make some feel like blocking out the world. On top of that is the day itself, a special meal which your child may or may not want to eat, plus the disappointment if presents do not match what was hoped for.

As the years have gone on, Sasha has withdrawn from all of these special days. One Mother's Day she ignored me for most of the day but then at bedtime asked if she could have a back massage. I laughed and pointed out that because it was Mother's Day maybe it was me who should be getting the back massage! Her reply to me was 'Oh yes. I think I had tuned Mother's Day out.' I know it has made her feel sad that she is not showing love in this way. In more recent years Sasha has not been able to wish anyone, not even me, her own mum, a happy birthday. I will admit that this upset me at first, but now I understand her reasons for not being able to show emotion as expected. It is not because she doesn't love me or because she doesn't care. I know she does, and I realize that I don't need a special occasion card or traditional greeting to show me that. It can feel difficult trying to explain this to other people though. To other parents who might be at the early stages of their 'journey' and who might feel upset by their children not producing cards or presents on special days, I think it helps to remember that it is just one day, and it is a day loaded with expectations. Ordinary, calmer days are more likely to be the times when your child feels more able to show their love or appreciation.

Anxiety

As she grew older, the ongoing high anxiety level that I associate with PDA seemed to remain for Sasha, but some of her specific fears and anxieties became more apparent. These are anxieties which you might find plenty of non-autistic people also struggling with – fear of flying because of 'what might happen', fear of natural disasters such as tornadoes or tsunamis, of alarm bells, house fires caused by electrical items and of being late and being looked at in public among others. Other fears such as spiders, flying things, being scratched by the cat or being approached by bouncy dogs are still fears but less concerning to Sasha; they are not taking over her life, they cause worry rather than extreme fear. It is important to note, though, that for some people these will not be small fears, they can be acute and debilitating.

Sasha has anxiety related to control in many other aspects of life and these are less like those common fears mentioned above. For years Sasha has had to sit in the front passenger seat and control the music in the car. We would have the same CD, her choice, on repeat for weeks or months at a time. There were only a limited number of songs that Sasha wanted to listen to; I became immune to the repetition, but Sasha's dad, Chris, would find it irritating and I am sure others would have found it unbearable if they had joined us regularly on our journey. At some point during our car journeys to school it became apparent that Sasha needed to listen to certain songs at a precise time in the journey. This would cause a huge upset when it just wasn't possible; even though Sasha would realize that the reason was simply the rate of traffic flow and we were not able to do anything to control that, she would still become distressed. When the chance to hear that song at a certain time had passed, because there had not been time for the previous song to finish, her train of thought was broken. She could not simply get over it and she was thrown into despair, which was very difficult to shift.

When she was younger, Sasha might have seemed easy-going to outsiders because we were so well versed in providing for her needs. Back then, she was less aware of potential issues (such as the unpredictable nature of weather) so they didn't cause her anxiety. As her understanding of the world developed, so did her fears, and one of her most used phrases was 'but there's still a slim chance!' of anything going wrong. She is no longer able to travel in an aeroplane because she worries there will be an accident, and she is scared to leave the house when there is any rain at all, worried there might be flooding. She used to refuse to go into school if she was late and would arrive in class after the other children, because they would then all look at her. These were not examples of her being oppositional for the sake of it, and they are not examples of her Pathological Demand Avoidance. My feeling is that these reactions are all down to general anxiety, but at a more extreme level than most.

Mental health

By the time she reached the age of eight, Sasha was becoming more aware of how having a meltdown made her stand out and look different to her peers. Being aware didn't make her any more able to not have meltdowns, it just contributed to Sasha feeling bad about herself.

The year after leaving her mainstream school was a difficult period emotionally for Sasha because she missed out on all the typical Year 6 rites of passage that her peers were experiencing. Last assemblies, the stage production, day trip to a theme park, leavers' parties and disco and, most notably, an outward-bound style trip away from home for a few days. Sasha was, and still is, desperate to take part in this type of activity like her peers, but she finds it hard to understand and process what challenges it might bring. She is excited by the idea of camaraderie, of being in a group, having fun. She is not able to appreciate what the impact on her of having to follow daily demands and instructions from others would be, and she has not yet managed to teach herself strategies to cope with all this.

After the breakdown of the MLD school placement, Sasha was gutted that it had all failed. In fact, she believed it was her fault because she had now failed at two schools. I tried to help her see how it was the environment at fault, not her. After some time at home, her mood recovered again and she was keen to try a different new school, realizing that the last one had not suited her. She accepted the extended time at home due to lockdowns during the pandemic because she was comfortable without the added pressure of interacting with others and being made to learn. But at the same time, she was looking forward to being able to find a new school setting where she could mix with others her own age. So when the next placement also failed, Sasha was devastated and went back to believing it was all her own fault. Sasha tried some art therapy at this stage, but although the therapist was great, Sasha did not feel able to express her worries in this way. She has a great vocabulary and is skilled with writing fiction, but has always found it very difficult to communicate with anyone verbally. She still struggles to have two-way conversations, even if it is about a topic that interests her. I worried that her mood was declining partly because she had not been able to talk about her experiences of the previous few years. Eventually though, she created an animated video which gave some insights into how she viewed her experiences at school. Giving her time to recover at home and allowing her to develop skills in her chosen areas of digital art and animation has helped to improve her self-esteem.

Apart from stressing that it is the 'little things' that matter, my other mantra is 'now is not forever'. As a parent, it is easy to worry about how your child is feeling or what your child is not able to do. I have felt frustrated about being stuck in a rut at times, but then I remind myself that usually, eventually, things do change. It might be hard to feel like we are not in control of the pace of change, but we can take a step back and think about how change feels for our children. Changing our mindset and thinking carefully about the demands and expectations we place upon our children can lead to more success for them in the future. In Chapter 11 I am going to explore some approaches that I found helped our family.

ADVICE FOR PARENTS AND CARERS

- Leaving the house:

    - When it comes to any activities outside of the house, planning for every eventuality we can think of often leads to more successful outcomes. Sometimes we just have to be on our toes though, ready to make a quick exit.

    - Removing the pressure of time can help some children find it easier to leave the house. Staying calm is also highly recommended!

    - Look for opportunities that involve your child's interests wherever possible.

    - Be prepared; consider items to take with you that can help regulate, whether that is technology, snacks and drinks, or sensory aids, such as ear defenders.

    - Acknowledge that trying to have whole-family outings or holidays and accommodating siblings' needs can sometimes create even more problems. Activities where a PDAer can have your undivided attention tend to run more smoothly.

- Sleep challenges:

    - Do whatever works for you and your family when it comes to setting a sleep routine. It is often a case of trial and error, and different solutions working at different ages and stages. Try to uncover the real issue – underlying anxieties are often at play and should be acknowledged. It is usually best to wait until you have restored your own energy levels before you try something new. But note too that things often change when you least expect them to!

- The PDA Society has written a very helpful sleep resource in conjunction with The Sleep Charity. On my website is a blog post that includes a variety of suggestions for solutions to help children get to sleep.[1]

- Special occasions:

  - Let it go. By this I mean reconsider what it is you are placing importance on, and why. Don't feel that you have to make your child wait for 'the big day' if you can see the excitement turning to stress and tension.

  - Look out for the signs. There are often signs before a child gets to the point of meltdown, even if they are subtle. Keep your eyes open and start reducing the number of activities that are happening if necessary; be flexible and alter your expectations accordingly.

  - Ask yourself 'does it matter?' Does it matter if your child doesn't follow society's expectations of what should happen on these occasions? Parents deserve a chance to relax once all the preparation has been done, but having stressed and unhappy children doesn't tend to be relaxing. In our house we lay a place at the Christmas table in the hope that our daughter feels like sitting down to join us, but there is no pressure on her to do so.

---

1   www.stephstwogirls.co.uk/2020/11/38-helpful-sleep-solutions-for-children.html

- Know your limits, and theirs. If you enjoy wrapping presents but they don't like the surprise of a wrapped gift, leave their gifts unwrapped and find someone else to wrap for. If one pile of presents all wrapped up neatly under the tree is too much tension, why not spread them out? If Christmas dinner is the most important part of Christmas day for you, and you feel you won't enjoy Christmas without everyone having sat at the table together for a certain length of time, then by all means state that as your wish. There is no guarantee it will be a happy occasion but only you will know if it is worth trying with your family.

- Anxiety:

  - Think about 'the little things'. Understanding what causes your child's anxiety levels to rise is the first step in helping them.

- Mental health:

  - If accessing private therapy for your child is an option, this might be worth considering but only if they are ready for it. There are different approaches that could be offered, from art or drama therapy to the more traditional talking therapy, but it is important to take note of what your child feels is helping them, and not forcing them to undergo therapy, especially if that is with adults who do not fully understand PDA. I suggest asking local charities or support groups for recommendations of providers and information on different types of therapy.

- – The NHS service that should be able to help with mental health is known as Children and Young People's Mental Health Services (CYPMHS) or Child and Adolescent Mental Health Services (CAMHS). Some, but not all, practitioners within this service may understand autism and the difficulties with mental health that sometimes arise alongside this diagnosis.

- Remember that now is not forever. Our children do learn new skills eventually. They all mature at different rates and the best approach we can take is to guide them rather than drag them through life.

Chapter 7
SENSORY ISSUES

A few years ago, the National Autistic Society shared a video from the point of view of somebody walking through a shopping centre. It gave an insight into how the senses of autistic people can end up being bombarded by noise and lights and sounds. I wrote a blog post at the time explaining that I imagined this was what Sasha experienced, but she was unable to express how she felt. I remember being amazed once when Sasha picked up on the noise of a video playing very quietly, from a long way away. She told me at the time that she can hear and feel everything. She reminded me of how she can often feel moisture in the air, so she knows when it's about to start raining before everyone else does. The teaching assistant who worked with Sasha in Junior school backed this up, remembering a few occasions when Sasha was not happy to go out to play even though it was dry outside. She soon realized that Sasha could sense the rain coming, because it always rained shortly after. Sasha wasn't able to explain what she was sensing though, so it was difficult for others to understand why she would not go out to play. We often joked about how she might make a great weather reporter when older!

We came to understand that some, but not all, of Sasha's reasons for avoidance were down to sensory issues. When she was young we would sometimes notice her freezing, clenching her jaw and tensing her whole body tightly and becoming rigid for a few seconds at a time. I remember mentioning this to the doctor, but it was waved off as nothing to worry about. Months after the autism diagnosis I attended a course about sensory profiles and it dawned on me that these clenching actions Sasha was doing might be fulfilling some kind of need for sensory input. Understanding more about sensory difficulties was enlightening and helped us to improve life for Sasha in some ways. We realized that her senses were struggling in all kinds of ways. Sudden noises, such as the hand dryers in public restrooms or alarm bells ringing, increased her anxiety levels quickly and could lead to a sensory overload that often resulted in meltdowns. Too much talking by others or any questions directed at her could have the same effect. All of these noises still have an impact now that she is 15, proving that the issues do not simply disappear over time.

We researched more about hyper- and hyposensitivity, trying to understand how Sasha's senses seemed to be both too acute (hypersensitivity) and not working at all (hyposensitivity). Sasha rarely complained of being ill, even when it was obvious to us that she had a fever or was showing signs of not being on top form. She seemed oblivious to having a cold, a high temperature, bumps or bruises. If she had a cut or a blister she often didn't seem to notice, but if one of these was really bothering her she would sometimes request a plaster. She would only leave a plaster on for a minute at most though, before getting upset and insisting it was removed. The feeling of anything unusual on her skin is unbearable to her, which explains why she will not leave plasters on for very long. She is also permanently hot and has an electric fan directed at her most of the time, day and night. She seems to have a higher body temperature than most people, and she has called herself 'a volcano on two legs', which made us laugh!

Dressing

Getting dressed was one of the main aspects of life where sensory issues were obvious from an early age. Sasha had just a few favourite items of clothing that she preferred to wear when leaving the house, one of them being a lovely blue flowery summer dress which she insisted on wearing all through the winter months. Putting on shoes had become a daily challenge; socks and tights were nearly always rejected. I remember feeling relieved when I managed to buy some soft fur-lined boots which would at least keep her feet slightly warmer in the winter without the socks. At the back of my mind was the thought that other parents would judge me for not making sure her feet were warm enough. If Sasha did agree to wear socks, they were never quite right for her and I would have to take them off and put them on again several times before we could leave the house. Another parent in one of the support groups I attended suggested seamless socks and these were a game changer for us. They were a great solution and one which we still use to this day.

When Sasha started at her new nursery, one of our biggest concerns was that children were supposed to wear a uniform and we were not sure if Sasha would agree to wear it. The uniform was only a polo shirt and soft tracksuit-style bottoms, but Sasha was already very particular about what clothes she would put on. At home she would wear very little most days, preferring not to have any clothing touching her skin. In later years, she slowly increased the amount of clothes she would wear outside, but the feeling of wearing a coat became an issue. We made it through a whole winter season with Sasha wearing only a thin hoodie rather than a waterproof coat; something I am sure many parents of teenagers might relate to, but this was before Sasha reached the age of ten. I learnt to cut labels out of most items and only bought Sasha clothes made from soft fabrics.

For several years she would only wear plain, short-sleeved stretchy jersey dresses. I would spend ages searching for dresses without embroidery, sequins, stitching or seams in different places, or any other kind of embellishment. The feeling of something unusual on her skin in a different place would cause her so much stress that she was unable to focus on anything else. On top of that, Sasha was also very particular about the colours she would wear, definitely no black or blue and she preferred pink as much as possible. All of this made shopping for her clothes and shoes a big (and ongoing) challenge for me!

Eating and drinking

Once she stopped drinking milk from baby bottles after her first year of life, Sasha would only ever drink water. No fruit juices, squash, fizzy drinks or milk. She always drank a lot of water during the day, and it was noticeable that if she didn't, her mood was affected. Sasha had a self-restricted diet even at a young age. She ate well, but from a repetitive list, at breakfast and lunchtime – always Weetabix, toast, bananas, sandwiches and cheese. Most days she refused all food at tea time, but very occasionally she would agree to pasta shapes from a tin and oven chips. Between the ages of three and four, Sasha somehow developed a love for Peperami sausages. No one else in our house likes to eat these and we can't remember how they became her favourite – possibly at a party or shared from another child's lunchbox. She loved Pringles crisps at this age too and I wondered if this was something to do with their uniform shape and texture. For a few months she ate the crisps as they were, but before long she moved onto simply licking the crisps, just to taste the flavour. Over time Sasha began to refuse some of the standard foods she had been happy with, which was worrying. One of the healthier foods she ate, Weetabix, had caused huge issues for us for many months. We would get frequent daily meltdowns over the fact that they were too soggy or too crispy, too much milk or not enough, and it was extremely difficult to serve it exactly how she liked it. She still wanted the Weetabix though. Bananas caused similar issues: too green or not green enough. Yellow bananas were never acceptable. So, in some ways, it was a relief when she dropped these from her diet.

Around that same period of time, I remember a day when, quite randomly and surprisingly, Sasha did eat two yellow (rather than still green) bananas though. It was a day of ups and downs; that was Sasha in a nutshell, full of contradictions. She could quickly go from one extreme to another in terms of her emotions. The day had started off fine, Sasha seemed content, but when it was time to take her big sister to school Sasha went off to try to put her own shoes on. She picked her 'pirate shoes' (pumps named so because they were red and went with her pirate outfit), which had been worn many times before. They had a Velcro strap across the top to hold them on. For some reason on that day Sasha tried to put these on without undoing the straps, and managed to do that with one foot, but when it came to the other foot she found she couldn't make it go in the pump.

At the first signs of distress, I offered to help Sasha with the pumps, but no, she was adamant she wanted to put them on herself, but without undoing the straps. She carried on battling, becoming more and more upset when she couldn't get her foot in. Each time I offered to help the screams got worse and she repeated over and over: 'No mummy help!' Meanwhile her older sister was sitting on the stairs, waiting unhappily with her hands over her ears. There was not much I could do, until Sasha eventually reached the point where she was so upset that she threw the shoes off. After what felt like hours, she let me hold her and cuddle her to calm down. She refused to put on any other shoes, so I had to carry her to the car with nothing on her feet. Making sure she didn't see, because I knew it would cause even more upset, I carefully put a pair of her sandals into the car to take with us rather than the pumps. By the time we got to school Sasha was calm again, and I managed to slide her sandals on without protest. Some might say that sounds like a typical toddler tantrum, but it was the intensity of the emotions and her extreme reactions that made this feel otherwise.

After dropping her big sister at school that day, Sasha suggested we go to the shops in town. Her request surprised me, because shopping was not usually something she enjoyed, even on a good day. Trips out to town were often cut short because Sasha would become overwhelmed by something, and it was often difficult to figure out what the triggers were. One thing that has stuck in my mind about how Sasha was back then is the fact she didn't have the typical toddler tantrums I would see other children having, including our older daughter. Although I initially worried about entering the local toy shop for fear of a big scene when we weren't able to buy anything new, Sasha would be quite happy to simply look at all the toy boxes, never asking for toys to be bought for her. All she ever wanted was a chocolate lollipop from the display at the till point, and that became part of our routine whenever we went to town. Tamsin would have tantrums occasionally when she wanted a toy, but she did accept a no from us fairly quickly and moved on. I sensed that it wouldn't have been quite so easy to move Sasha on if she was determined to have something for whatever reason, so I was relieved when she didn't expect anything big to be bought for her. Back to the yellow bananas story – that day after the stressful school drop off, we had an unexpected but lovely hour just wandering round the shops with no pressure and brilliant, calm behaviour from Sasha. She asked to go to a food shop, specifically for bananas, she picked out two yellow ones and then promptly ate them. An act that has never been repeated!

One of the first big hurdles when Sasha started school was

lunchtime and working out what she could eat. Her diet had become very repetitive and she would only eat a limited number of foods. In many aspects of life, she had a fear of trying anything new, whether at home or at school, and that applied to food too. In the school dinner hall, there were so many stress factors. She struggled to cope with a lot of noise, or with strong smells. On top of that, queuing for anything was difficult because Sasha seemed to lack patience, but also because being so near to other young children who might jostle and bump into her caused her to become distressed. I knew school was not the ideal time or place for Sasha to try new foods, but I also knew she would not eat anything we put in a packed lunch. We had tried giving her sandwiches at picnics or when travelling, but despite loving them at home, she always refused them when we were out of the house. In later years Sasha was able to tell us that the plastic boxes, the cling film or the foil had their own specific tastes that would be passed on to the sandwiches so she could not eat them.

We signed Sasha up for school dinners and crossed our fingers that it would work out. The school cook and her team were amazing and really helped. They took Sasha under their wing and made the accommodations she needed in terms of food and how it was served to her. We discovered fairly quickly that Sasha liked the potatoes at school but wouldn't eat much else that was on offer – a bit of plain chicken very occasionally, and jelly, but only if it was orange or strawberry flavour. Sasha still misses the school potatoes. It didn't matter how I tried to recreate them at home, they were never quite the same.

One of my fondest memories from the time of transition to Junior school was when the cook from Infant school let me know that she had been to visit the kitchen staff at the Junior school. She had taken the time to make a special trip of her own accord, to talk to them all about Sasha. She had typed up a whole sheet for them, about what Sasha liked to eat and how she liked to be served it. It was full of tips of how she had been helping Sasha to cope: the foods Sasha did like (potatoes) and didn't like (pretty much everything else – 'will not eat cake, fruit or yoghurt'), and how the potatoes should be cooked ('lightly, crispy but not at all burnt'). There was also an issue around certain bowls which Sasha would not eat out of. Sasha wasn't able to articulate the exact problem but we assumed the smell of the plastic was the reason. The cook had come up with other options and detailed these on her instruction sheet too.

It warmed my heart to see how much time and effort the cook put into looking after Sasha, and to see how much she wanted the transition to be a success. At the bottom of the sheet she had typed 'Thank you for looking after Sasha', and it made me think about Paddington Bear: 'Please look after this Bear. Thank you.' It was so kind and helpful and I was so grateful. It was a tiny bit bittersweet, as I knew none of the other children needed that kind of information sheet or support; however, the positives far outweighed that feeling and this act of kindness was both one I have never forgotten, and one that I know made a huge difference in terms of helping Sasha. It showed real compassion, and more than that, an understanding of how important the details were to help make things run smoothly. On the first day of Junior school Sasha didn't eat any lunch at all because the dining room was too overwhelming for her. Plans were quickly put in place to help Sasha at lunchtime, including being matched up with a buddy from her class who would help her go up to the counter for the food and then sit with her to eat. This ensured that Sasha got to eat her beloved school potatoes, most of the time. She has still never eaten any potatoes for me at home though!

One time Sasha was invited to a birthday party for one of her classmates and there was party food on offer after the main event. I was watching from a short distance away as the children all sat at a table and one mum started passing round trays of sandwiches. My eyes opened wide as Sasha leant forward and took a ham sandwich in brown bread from the tray and started eating it. Not only that, but she ate it all, crusts included! Of course, I had tried to give Sasha a variety of food at home, including sandwiches made in different kinds of bread, and when I started making sandwiches for her I did not initially cut the crusts off, but we had reached a point where she would only eat white bread sandwiches with a cheese spread on, and only if the top and bottom crusts were cut off. So, to see her eat something else at a party was a surprise, but again an act that was never to be repeated at home or even at any other parties following that one. Was she just extra hungry that day? Or was it the novelty factor? I will never know, because her communication skills were not good enough to tell me.

Over the past few years, we have made several attempts to increase the variety in Sasha's diet but very few new foods have ever been added. She currently eats the same eight items every day. She is tall and healthy though and it would seem her body does a good job of fighting off most infections. I don't spend every day trying to convince her to eat new food items because that would be exhausting and, in my experience, fairly fruitless. I try to revisit the idea of her trying new food at times when she is feeling most relaxed. A couple of years ago we introduced 'Taste Test Tuesdays'; I would buy some random new food from the supermarket for Sasha to try or she would suggest something she fancied. It was her idea that this should happen on a Tuesday; she has always been a fan of puns, alliteration and word games. I would put the new food on a plate, put a blindfold on Sasha (again, her idea) and, with a dash of humour, do my best to persuade her to try the food. Most of the new items were only licked, or at best given a tiny nibble. The novelty of this game wore off after a few weeks. It might seem an easy option for me to serve the same foods to Sasha every day, but I find it boring and I would definitely rather be serving her a wider variety of

PDA IN THE FAMILY

home-cooked food. She eats what she can cope with eating for now, and although this issue of food has caused a great deal of stress over the years, I have had to learn to relax and not worry about it too much. If I worry that others might think I am being lazy, I remind myself that they do not see what goes on behind the scenes in our house.

I have never liked the term 'fussy eater'. I can eat a wide range of foods myself but there are definitely some foods that I prefer and eat more regularly than others and I imagine that applies for the vast majority of people. Selective is a kinder way of putting it, rather than fussy. It might be true that for some children they will eat what they are given, and if you refuse to give them anything else they will eventually eat what you want them to eat, but this definitely did not apply to our child. Sasha would rather have eaten nothing than be forced to eat what she did not want.

Whilst on the subject of food, I probably should mention Sasha's favourite... McDonalds. I am not sure how old Sasha was when she tasted her first 'fry' or whose decision it was to take her there, but McDonalds fries on a Saturday teatime have become an integral part of our life. The order for Sasha was always three medium fries, brought home to eat with the sliced turkey and cucumber that are part of her daily evening meal every other day. One time she decided to try a hamburger to go with her fries but she only took the tiniest of nibbles before letting us know that she couldn't eat it. The first UK lockdown due to the global pandemic in March 2020 brought huge stress to our house, when McDonalds closed their doors and we were unable to provide Sasha with her regular Saturday fries. We tried everything to replicate the fries at home; we purchased a deep fat fryer and an air fryer and worked our way through every brand of chip for fryer or oven. We even made a special trip to a McDonalds outlet the night before they closed, to take delivery of some of their own frozen fries in the vain hope that we could cook them in a way that would replicate the standard McDonalds taste. It didn't work. Sasha's mood was extremely low for that nine-week period when McDonalds was closed. When McDonalds began to offer a delivery service before their stores were able to re-open, it sadly wasn't available in our local area. A very kind friend of ours who lives near a McDonalds that was doing delivery offered to order some fries to her house on Sasha's behalf. I drove half an hour to collect them from her house. They were of course cold by the time we got them home, but after a quick warm up in the oven they were declared 'ok' by Sasha. We all celebrated the day when the McDonalds' drive-thrus reopened. Having the Saturday routine back as it used to be improved Sasha's mood hugely. As an added bonus, Sasha decided that it was time she should try a new food item from the McDonalds menu. She plumped for a mayo chicken burger, plain, and I know some parents will understand my happiness about that now being a regular item in the order for Sasha!

Health and medicine

From a very young age Sasha refused all kinds of medicine. She would put up a big struggle if we approached her with any Calpol or Nurofen, knocking spoons or cups out of our hands, and she quickly realized if we tried to cheat by hiding any medicine in her food. We couldn't add medicine to her water (she never drinks anything flavoured) because we knew she would notice the altered taste. On the odd occasion we did manage to get any medicine into her when she was very young, she would gag and regurgitate it. Totally the opposite reaction to our older daughter, who would have drunk Calpol like it was going out of fashion, given half a chance! Attempting to give Sasha medicine seemed to cause her more upset and stress than whatever it was the medicine was trying to help with.

When she was around five years old, I took Sasha to the doctor with a case of tonsillitis. He suggested prescribing antibiotics and I replied that there was no point because she wouldn't take them if he did. He looked at me dumbfounded and asked 'but what would you do if she was really ill?!' and I had to admit that I didn't know. At that point in time, I was hoping he had an answer for me rather than the other way about. Her condition did worsen a few days later and we were sent to A&E. My worst memory of that time was that it took four nurses to hold Sasha down to insert a cannula to enable her to have the antibiotics intravenously.

In May 2016, when she was nine years old, Sasha had a bad cough and didn't eat any food for four days. We went to see our doctor, who suggested it was a virus, so when Sasha started eating again we assumed she was getting better. Her temperature kept going up and down, but nothing extremely alarming, so we concluded she was simply suffering from the virus. A week later Sasha looked a bit puffy, so we visited another doctor who informed us Sasha had an ear infection. Despite it clearly being a bad infection, Sasha hadn't complained of any pain. We administered the prescribed ear drops and hoped they would help her recover.

Three days later Sasha was physically sick in the morning, and by the evening the puffiness/swelling in her face had worsened. I called an out of hours doctor, concerned, even though Sasha didn't seem to be bothered in any way by how she looked or felt. We got an appointment for 9.30pm; Sasha did not want to go and I had to work hard to persuade her. We set off with her beloved soft toy and a bucket and towel in case she felt sick again. I left the bucket in the car but fortunately took the towel with me as we went in to see the doctor... because no sooner had we sat down than Sasha threw up again, into my towel-covered arms. The doctor seemed slightly confused because all Sasha's indicators were reading typical – no raised temperature, blood pressure standard, breathing normal, etc.

When he heard how long she had been off colour for, he decided the best course of action would be to send us straight to A&E.

Sasha was fairly calm and resigned to the adventure as I drove her to the hospital. The next five hours in A&E felt like days. We spent a couple of hours sitting on one chair, waiting to be seen. Eventually, we were relieved to be given a bed to lie on and they began to try to establish what was wrong. An X-ray was taken after the first couple of hours' wait, and the results that were brought back a couple of hours later showed her chest had fluid on it. So it was decided antibiotics would be a good course of action. By now it was around one o'clock in the morning and I had to try to give Sasha some very strong-smelling white 'stuff' in a syringe. I think Sasha partly agreed to take the medicine because she was just too tired to resist but also because the doctor told me, and so I told Sasha, that if she took the medicine we would be allowed to go home.

I was surprised when I managed to get the medicine down her. I spent the following hour feeling relieved, whilst wondering how long it would take them to discharge us. When the doctor returned though, she informed me she now thought it might be pneumonia. She wanted to give more antibiotics and fluids via a cannula and a drip, and then transfer us to a ward. Sasha was still refusing to take any other medicine (paracetamol or ibuprofen) and of course I was worried about her, but I was also sad that I had to break my promise about going home when she had managed to take the medicine. I had not made any allowance for the doctor changing her mind, or for the fact that Sasha might be very ill, and I did not like having to go back on my word to Sasha. Her limited understanding of the situation made it difficult to explain why we were having to stay.

That was just the beginning though. Sasha stayed in hospital for ten days while they tried to discover what was wrong, and I stayed with her. After the first day or two during which Sasha was visited, prodded and asked questions by several different doctors and nurses, I realized I needed to become stronger at protecting her from the intrusions. Sasha has always hated any questions being asked of her, largely because she finds it so difficult to communicate to answer them. So I had to make sure questions were directed at me, out of Sasha's earshot whenever possible, and I also created a short information document to help let others know about her autism and PDA diagnosis. Sasha must have been tired, frightened and confused, and I was exhausted. The worst moment of our stay was when Sasha had to have a computerized tomography (CT) scan. Luckily, thanks to the CBeebies programme *Get Well Soon*, she had watched a video about having a CT scan some months prior to our stay in hospital, so at least she was a little prepared about what might happen. It was still an immensely stressful experience. The day after that we had to face a long journey: a transfer in an ambulance to the Royal Brompton Hospital in London so they could do heart scans. Due to the local team calling ahead with information about Sasha, a friendly play therapist greeted us when we arrived and helped prepare her for the electrocardiogram test. She also printed a sheet for the door of the room we were in, letting staff know that it was best not to ask Sasha questions directly. We were given a separate room rather than a bed on a noisy general ward and I think it is fair to say that both the room and the play therapist contributed in a big way to Sasha's recovery.

The final verdict on the cause of the illness was Post Streptococcal Glomerulonephritis, a rare kidney disease after a bacterial infection. Thankfully, the medicine worked well eventually and we were both relieved to leave the hospital ten days later. In all that time, one of the most difficult things was trying to explain to Sasha how the hospital was helping and why she should be there. As far as Sasha was concerned, she wasn't even feeling particularly ill when we ended up in A&E, and all the hospital was doing was making her feel worse! She still refuses all medicine at home if she is ever feeling poorly and we have come to accept that she is lucky that her body naturally fights off most infections. After hospital, Sasha skipped happily back into school as if she had never been away.

Personal hygiene

Self-care and personal hygiene tasks are laden with demands and this is an aspect of life that Sasha has always found challenging. Brushing teeth is a task that Sasha has done her best to avoid from a very early age. As with lots of other daily life tasks, we found that whilst our eldest daughter had no problem with following the suggested morning and evening routine that we taught her, Sasha seemed to find it difficult for some reason. It began to turn into a daily battle before leaving for school in the morning and again at bedtime, so we looked for solutions. For a while we used a fun teeth brushing app that consisted of a timer with a fun song to dance along to as teeth were brushed. There were extra points of interest in the app, such as being able to select different outfits for the characters. The novelty factor won again, but as with everything this only worked for a while for Sasha.

We feel extremely lucky to have found a great dentist when our girls were younger, someone who took the time to understand Sasha's needs and act accordingly. He is fun and chatty at a level that suits Sasha and he has never admonished her for what she is not able to do. Going for a regular check-up is something she tolerates rather than enjoys, but she has never tried to avoid going and I put this down to her liking the good relationship she has with him. Sasha's teeth and gums have always been perfectly healthy considering all the brushing they have missed out on – we put this down to the fact that she only drinks water and doesn't eat sweets!

In the years that followed we have tried a range of different ideas, from differently flavoured or even tasteless toothpaste to a variety of toothbrush styles. Nothing makes much difference for long though, because tooth brushing is an act that Sasha finds too difficult. If you ask her why, she will reply that it is because it is boring and a waste of her time, but we know this is not the full picture. Part of the issue is sensory problems – how the brushes feel in her mouth and how the toothpaste tastes – but the other factor we have to consider is the expectation that she should be brushing her teeth. She knows she should do it, but that makes it all the more difficult. This actually applies to most aspects of looking after her own body and health, and we know she is not alone with this. We have spoken with many parents of PDA children and even adults who experience this; but of course, it is worth bearing in mind that it does not mean that all individuals will have this same struggle.

ADVICE FOR PARENTS AND CARERS

- Explore sensory profiles:

  - Consider that avoidance might be down to sensory issues. There are many different sensory products, but it helps to understand what specific items might help your child. Sensory-friendly clothing such as seamless socks, or tops and shoes that fasten with Velcro, fidget tools, light toys, ear defenders, chewable items or weighted blankets are just a few examples of what is available.

- Eating issues:

  - Food caused a lot of stress in our house in the early years. Our daughter has stayed relatively healthy though, so I gradually came to accept that she must be choosing foods that are right for her and that give her the nutrients she needs. Don't let those fixed ideas of what makes a healthy meal weigh heavily on you as a parent all the time.

– However, if you are concerned about children who are struggling to eat a good variety of foods, it might be worth researching ARFID (Avoidant Restrictive Food Intake Disorder).

• Medicine:

– If anyone knows of a way to make a child take medicine, I am all ears! On my blog there is a post sharing lots of suggestions of how to persuade children to take medicine. I have had great feedback about some of the ideas working well, but sadly none of them ever worked for us.

• Hospital. I was not prepared in any way for our hospital stay but I definitely learnt from the experience. My advice for other parents would be:

– Create a one-page profile, an easy-to-read document that will explain to doctors and nurses what could help your child in terms of communication and environment. Giving information about their likes/dislikes and previous health history can help. There are templates online if you search for hospital passport, healthcare passport, one-page profile, or any combination of those words. Keep a copy of this on your phone so you are prepared in an emergency.

– Remember you know your child best. If they are unable

to answer questions from strangers, don't feel that you should politely let the healthcare professionals keep asking your child rather than you. If, conversely, you think your child is capable of answering and you would rather questions were directed at them rather than you, let staff know that.

— Do not be too shy or polite to ask for help. There might be a play therapist assigned to the hospital, someone who is trained to help children understand what is happening. Or you might find there is support for you as a parent; in the first hospital I was at with our girl, there was a carer support team who were so kind, bringing me cups of tea or sitting with her for a few minutes while I went to have a shower. They made a huge difference to me.

- Personal hygiene:

   — Accept that this can be an aspect of daily living that some PDAers will have difficulty with. Reduce the demands, and offer choices or help with them whenever possible.

   — Other parents will have many suggestions of ways to help, and as with other issues, it is definitely worth asking for further advice via your support networks.

Chapter 8
SIBLINGS, FAMILY AND FRIEND RELATIONSHIPS

As much as I try to be positive about everything most of the time, there is no denying that living with a PDAer can be difficult for everyone. It has a big impact on relationships in all sorts of ways. One of the questions I am asked most often is how to help siblings of PDA children. The reason my blog is titled *Steph's Two Girls* is because one of my first thoughts on hearing that Sasha was to be diagnosed autistic was that the news would also have a big impact on our older daughter's life. At that age they were getting on well with each other, in much the same way I did with my siblings. I certainly remember our girls spending lots of time together, and I have videos showing much fun and laughter when we were all at home together. Life was always more difficult when we were out of the house though, for reasons I have explained earlier. When I chose the name for my blog, I wanted people to realize that it wasn't all about Sasha, although eventually most of the writing did end up being about her reactions to different situations. I think I felt concern for Tamsin because I knew the autism diagnosis for Sasha would mean there would always be something different about Tamsin's life too, but that most people wouldn't stop to consider how she felt about it all.

One example of this came soon after Sasha started at school. Tamsin informed me that there had been an incident at lunchtime, when Sasha had ended up distressed over something. Nobody was quite sure what had caused the upset, but it had led to a full-on meltdown in the dining hall. Tamsin had seen meltdowns many times at home but was somewhat embarrassed to see it happen in the middle of the school dining hall, with friends asking her what Sasha was doing. Sasha was blocking the path of other children, so one of the members of staff asked Tamsin if she was able to help calm and move her sister. Tamsin told me that she had tried, but without much success. I think this aspect of a sibling relationship should be approached carefully by those in education. It would have been great for everyone if Tamsin did know how to help Sasha in that situation, but there was no doubt that being asked to help added extra pressure and embarrassment for Tamsin that day.

Tamsin was brilliant with Sasha when they were younger and I think Sasha appreciates this even now. It is clear that Tamsin holds a special place in Sasha's heart and that Sasha will always love her. Although we didn't make a point of sitting Tamsin down to tell her about Sasha's diagnosis in any great detail, we never hid it from her either. We did mention that Sasha was autistic but Tamsin was only approaching five years old at the time Sasha was diagnosed, so I am not sure how much of that sank in. We would talk about how Sasha found it difficult to do certain things, or tried to explain when Sasha couldn't understand or when she was behaving in a way that might not be typically expected. We didn't need to labour the point though, because Tamsin seemed to instinctively understand what Sasha needed and she began to use the same kind of approaches with her sister that we used. We didn't have to suggest to Tamsin that she act in a certain way around Sasha, she was just quick to realize what the outcome would be if she didn't bend and allow her sister control in most situations. That is not to say there were never any clashes or that the usual sibling rivalry has not happened over the years, but on the whole Tamsin has been amazing in her efforts to make things work. We have tried to give her quality time and different experiences in an attempt to make things more even, but we are aware this does not replace having the typical family experiences that she might otherwise have had.

When Sasha was around seven, I remember trying to take both girls to see the Disney *Cars* movie at the cinema. I thought Sasha would enjoy it but we all had to leave after ten minutes because she couldn't bear it. She wasn't able to express why, but I wondered whether it was because the film started off with a lot of loud, fast action, with all the cars racing. Or maybe it was the idea of talking cars that seemed so strange and alien to her. Often, it was difficult to figure out what the problem was for Sasha. That day, not for the first time, I felt sad for our eldest daughter because she would have liked to stay and watch the movie. But because I was on my own with the girls and Tamsin was young, I couldn't leave her there alone. Having to leave places early happened a lot in those years and I was always thinking of and worrying about the impact on Tamsin. It was a fine balance, because I hoped she could have the experiences that other children had, so I didn't want her to have to just stay home. However, I also knew that if we tried to stay at any place where Sasha was not happy then a very loud and public meltdown would ensue. I could see the level of embarrassment that having other people stare at us caused Tamsin, so I tried to avoid that as much as possible.

Another time we decided on a family outing to the cinema to watch the newly released film *Secret Life of Pets*. Another animation, with cute animals, and Sasha had loved the *My Little Pony* movie, so I assumed this film would be a good choice. Again, only ten minutes into the movie, Sasha had had enough and I had to leave the cinema with her while Tamsin stayed to watch the film with her dad. Because we had all travelled there in one car, I had to spend the next hour-and-a-half sitting outside the cinema while Sasha watched her iPad. She was annoyed she couldn't go home straight away, but I was determined that Tamsin would get to stay and enjoy the whole movie (and I was relieved that I had thought to bring the iPad along in case this happened!).

When asked about how she felt growing up with Sasha, Tamsin talks about how she often had to compromise in order to prevent big meltdowns, and that she was aware that Sasha never compromised. She remembers how she always gave up the front seat of the car for Sasha, and always had to let Sasha listen to her choice of music in the car. Tamsin knew that if she didn't let Sasha have her way it would cause a massive meltdown, but she also realized that she wouldn't have that same extreme reaction herself, so she could see the difference in emotion. When Sasha stopped going to school, Tamsin didn't understand why exactly, but because she was happy going to school herself it didn't make her want to stay home and avoid it. All of these things did understandably make life feel unfair for Tamsin though.

It makes me sad to reflect on how the way we have lived has affected Tamsin too, but I still believe that we all did what we had to do to make life manageable. Since Sasha left the mainstream school at the age of nine, she has not had friends to interact with. One reason for that is because she finds communication and the give and take of relationships too difficult to navigate, and another is that she only wants to converse with others about her own special interests. So, when Sasha was younger, we did sometimes ask Tamsin to fill this gap that friends would have otherwise occupied. We suggested she spend some time playing Minecraft or other computer games with her sister. Or we gently encouraged her to play with us all together as a family. Family gaming was not without issues though. There is a fairly basic concept of give and take, or compromising, that children tend to pick up when they are young. Despite attempts from us, from Early Years Autism Support and from school staff to teach Sasha this, it seemed as if she would never grasp this kind of cooperation and reciprocity. Sasha needed to control, and win, all games. She could not bear not winning the game. We would experience huge meltdowns if we didn't let Sasha win, or if we didn't play a game to her own, made-up rules. Tamsin might not have liked losing games but it didn't cause the same over-reactions and upset that we saw from Sasha, and Tamsin never tried to control the games to suit herself. We would try to play interactive multiplayer games as a family, but more often than not, they ended in tears.

One time Sasha walked by as her dad and I were playing Cluedo with her older sister. We knew that if we had originally asked Sasha to join in, she would have said no, but in any case we were using the opportunity to have some quality time with our older daughter. Curiosity got the better of Sasha though and she suddenly decided that she did want to join in. So, we went through the painstaking task of trying to explain the rules to her and then began playing whilst trying to ensure that Sasha did not feel like she was losing the game at any point. What that meant was that the rest of us were not having much fun at all, but it just about worked for Sasha, so we felt quietly pleased that we had been able to do a group activity. A week later, we suggested it again (that was our first mistake!). As we set the board up, Sasha asked for a refresh of the rules because she was feeling muddled. Tamsin and I tried to run through them but Sasha was convinced in her mind that what we were saying (about proposing a weapon, person and room every time) was not right. She was sure we only had to say one of those things each time. So, we gently tried to explain the game rules again, but it started to dawn on me that we were talking too much and it was all too complicated for her. I tried to think on my feet and reduce the demands, suggesting we could play the game in whatever way Sasha wanted, even though I knew that Tamsin would find it more difficult because it would make the game ten times longer and she was not keen on playing with her sister in the first place, but it was too late.

Sasha went very tense, ran back to the sofa to hide under her duvet and screamed at us to leave the room. Then she ran upstairs to her bedroom for what was for a time her standard meltdown routine. She slammed the bedroom door, threw everything off her bed and wrapped herself up in her duvet – to the point where she became extremely hot and sweaty. She would also often leave us a message on the small lightbox outside her room, warning us not to enter the room, or telling us how much she hated us. 'Muck your femory' was what appeared on the lightbox that day; Sasha trying to tell us that we had remembered the rules wrong (clearly we hadn't, but it is very unusual for her to not remember something perfectly, so I did wonder where the confusion had crept in). There was not much we could do when she was in the meltdown state; after leaving her for a while to calm down I would go in, lie next to her and hug her, whilst saying very little. Occasionally she would apologize afterwards, knowing her outbursts were unreasonable, but she was unable to control them.

I think that although Sasha understands that there needs to be give and take in various aspects of life, she still struggles with being able to let that happen. She still needs to control, and win, any games. Even though she knows that is not a good way to act, because it means nobody wants to play those games with her, she has to accept that because she knows that she can't bear not winning the game. As Sasha got older and able to explain how she felt about playing games, she told us that it was not about being ultra-competitive, it was about anxiety and loss of control. For a long time, we had a shelf full of board games that we were not able to play, but I somehow found myself unable to give them away. I think that was something to do with them feeling like a symbol of what a typical family might have, and might be able to enjoy together.

I have since come to the conclusion that families who experience only happy times while playing board games are probably in the minority! However, at the time I wished our older daughter could experience that kind of fun family activity. Tamsin tried so hard to be accommodating for her younger sister and I always appreciated her efforts. I could see how unfair and frustrating the situation was for her, but we were unable to change Sasha's thought process. We reached a point where we consciously decided to not ask Tamsin to interact with her sister. Giving them both their own space was the best we could do for both of them. We are sure they will come together to figure out their relationship when they are ready, in their own time, on their own terms.

Sasha is different to many of her peers and that makes relationships with other children difficult for her. She is not keen to converse about anything much unless it is around one of her interests. She could talk a lot about Nintendo games, such as Mario, Kirby or Splatoon, or Skylanders or Steven Universe. She has a great memory and can identify pretty much every one of the 800+ Pokémon characters, but she has no interest in make-up or music or shopping for example, and she is not able to listen to others talk about these kinds of topics. Sasha would find it difficult to go on any outing that other teenagers of her age might do. Shopping, bowling, golf, parties, the cinema... lots of social interaction and unknowns are involved with these types of activities. She has only ever watched a handful of films at the cinema, with *Inside Out*, *Trolls* (this was such a hit that we went to see it three times at the cinema), and most recently *Encanto* giving her the most enjoyment. She originally rejected the idea of going to see *Encanto* because she was adamant she is not a Disney fan, but a few weeks later she came across a couple of clips of it on YouTube, and she fell in love with some of the music from the film. Her favourite song is Surface Pressure, probably because it is a great song but also because she relates to the lyrics. Music has played such a big part in her enjoyment of anything over the years.

Going to the cinema is an excursion full of demands, not least the pressure of getting there for a certain time, for when the movie is scheduled to begin, so it is no wonder that we haven't achieved it that often. But there are not many films that Sasha has agreed to watch at home in her safe space either. She has always been very definite about what she will and won't watch. I used to wonder if it was because she found it too difficult to understand many of the plot lines, or if she got bored too easily, and this might have been the case when she was younger. Recently she has managed to give us a different explanation though. All the films she has ever watched have been animations, including the handful that she has watched at home. Sasha won't watch movies with 'real life' people in them, and she gives 'because all people are ugly' as her reason. I asked her if what she actually meant by this had something to do with the idea that some autistic people are said to find eye contact difficult. Her response was: 'I don't understand why not making eye contact is considered rude. What makes people think that not looking at someone means they are not listening? It's more beneficial to not look so you can focus on something else at the same time. Multitasking is a thing, people!'

Sasha has told us a few times recently that she doesn't like real people at all. This is hard to hear, especially as she was such a happy, sociable child when younger. I try not to dwell on this too much, assuming that being a teenager and the hormones associated with this time of life are playing a part in her comments. The past couple of years with the pandemic situation have certainly not helped, and neither have the breakdowns of her school placements. Relationships have always been difficult for many reasons. But I don't think she really dislikes everyone, and I am hopeful that as an adult she will feel more comfortable around other people again.

Sasha will also tell us that the iPad is her life, and that she thinks she has been brought up by the Internet. I console myself with the knowledge that this is definitely not true. Up until the age of ten, Sasha had attended the mainstream school full-time with pretty good attendance levels. Thanks in part to my blog, we also had a fairly active and varied life at weekends, with opportunities to take part in unusual experiences such as film premieres or the Moshi Monsters party or a launch event for Nintendo games. These might not have been plain sailing, but we did attempt many different outings despite having to often leave early. Sasha was not at home, stuck to a screen the whole time. I was having to work much harder than parents of most neurotypical children in terms of planning for any time spent out of the house; I can say this with the knowledge of having an older daughter who we did not have to make these extra plans for. I wanted my children to enjoy varied experiences though, so I made the effort to embrace those opportunities we were given.

This year I celebrated a milestone birthday and I would have loved to hold a big party at our house, to bring together all our friends and family. I couldn't bring myself to do it though, because I would have felt on edge the whole time, knowing the detrimental effect that having lots of people in our home and the party atmosphere would have had on Sasha. That is not to say I wouldn't consider it at some point in the future if we found a way to make it manageable for Sasha, but for now, I am happy putting her needs first. Other group occasions/celebrations are also difficult. Our neighbours held a garden party for the Jubilee celebrations and my husband Chris and I popped in for some celebrating and socializing. This is the kind of family event that I would have wished our girls to be a part of too, but they just don't work for Sasha and we have had to accept that. It can sometimes feel difficult for us to see other children at these kinds of events, enjoying themselves in a seemingly easy way. We would love to experience the feeling of other people seeing our girls enjoying themselves as part of a community, but we know such events would be unbearable for Sasha.

Earlier this year, my younger brother got married and I was not sure whether Sasha would agree to be at the wedding. Part of the difficulty was the fact that the venue was a three-hour drive away, but it probably would have been equally problematic if it had been taking place in the town where we lived. Nobody tried to force Sasha to attend; as mentioned earlier we have always felt well supported by family members and they understood why an occasion like this would be difficult for her. Sasha wanted to be there though, so the demand and expectation was really coming from within. We were all pleased when she joined us on the day, managing to overcome her anxieties over travel and the event itself; we appreciated the effort she had had to make. I think for many people these kinds of celebrations are considered fun events that we don't think twice about attending. All the sensory and socializing aspects were just too overwhelming for Sasha on the day. She managed to sit through the wedding celebration ceremony itself, although it helped that it was relatively short. It also helped that the meal and disco that followed were in the same building because I don't think Sasha would have stayed for as long as she did if we had had to transfer elsewhere. Chris and I spent the whole meal taking it in turns to carry our plates of food out of the main reception room, to sit with Sasha in a side room where she was trying to find a quiet spot away from all the other guests. She became progressively more upset about the situation; some of that was driven by the fact that she wanted to be able to be like everyone else and enjoy the whole event. She simply was not able to cope, despite wanting to. I would have dearly loved to feel relaxed and be able to properly enjoy my brother's wedding, catching up with family and friends, but it just wasn't possible. The same applied when other friends and family have had barbecues or parties or any other kind of get-together; we have missed out on many fun, social events because of the difficulties that Sasha experiences with everyday life. I feel bad for writing this though, because I absolutely do not want Sasha to feel that any of this was her fault.

On a similar train of thought, seeing Sasha's peers and even sister carrying on with their typical lives and passing major milestones can bring home to us how different her life is. It can be all too easy to feel envious and experience a twinge in the heart at the fact that those children have friends, enjoy parties and go on sleepovers, are rewarded at school for good attendance, are awarded grades in exams, have driving lessons, go to University or college and so on. This does not mean that we begrudge the happiness and achievements of those children. We are, of course, pleased for them and their parents, and thrilled at the achievements of our older daughter. But the typical events that happen during the period of school years are a constant reminder of having a child whose life is on a different path to the one expected. That doesn't make it a terrible path (although at times the battles with the system can certainly make parents feel that way), it just means that it takes some time to get used to the idea of everything being different, and it can be hard for other parents to relate to our experiences. Sasha herself doesn't pay too much attention to what other people are doing, so she is not bothered about not going to prom, or not taking driving lessons, and very definitely not bothered about not taking exams! We are not disappointed with her at all, we don't feel she is failing, we think she is doing a great job of being herself. But I think we do have occasional feelings of sadness that she is not getting the chance to achieve milestones like this.

When you have children who are different, I think it is fair to say that your circle of friends becomes much smaller. Most of us are drawn to spending time with other people who just 'get it', so that we don't have to keep explaining ourselves. The ones who are living similar lives and who can sympathize. What we definitely do not need in our already stressful lives is judgemental people who think they could do a better job. We have been so lucky to have unconditional support from all our family, but I have heard from many other parents that sadly that is not always the case. Some relationships are worth keeping, so it might be necessary to find neutral ground, gently educating and reminding other family members what you have already tried in terms of parenting. Keep in mind that you are the parent, you are the one who spends the most time with the child and you are the one that knows the child best. Finding a support system made up of people who truly understand the challenges is definitely something I recommend, but it is worth remembering that even those who are not walking in your shoes can still be caring and compassionate. Our closest friends have been so supportive and have given us the strength to carry on through the tougher times.

I would never have been described as the life and soul of the party; I am quiet rather than outgoing, but I am sociable and I do love people. I love watching them, being around them, and interacting with them. Thinking about my own childhood, I definitely lacked confidence and may have had some degree of social anxiety, but that didn't stop me wanting to be a part of anything. During the last five years when Sasha hasn't been regularly attending school, I have spent a lot of time in my own house. I have to limit what work I can agree to outside of the home so that I am here for Sasha most of the time. Socializing with other adults only happens with a great deal of consideration and planning. I appreciate how lucky I am to be part of a couple so that cover for me can sometimes be arranged though, and my heart goes out to single parent families who find this aspect of life difficult.

I am living a different life to the one I thought I would have, but to be honest it is weird how many of us expect certain things from life in the first place. No one has a working crystal ball, after all. Lots of people end up having lives that are different to what they expected, for a whole multitude of reasons. I will admit to having had feelings of disappointment and regret about what I was not able to do at times, particularly during the first few years after Sasha's diagnosis. But I like to think I am a glass half-full kind of girl; I don't believe that negative emotions do much to help make life better, so I don't dwell on any of this now. Making the most of the life I have is definitely my plan for the foreseeable future.

In the days, weeks and months after autism was first mentioned, I threw myself into learning everything I could about it. I attended parenting courses, I went to conferences, I had a big stack of books on the subject of autism by the side of my bed (still do) and I spent many late nights researching every article I could find online. I found it frustrating that Chris did not seem to want to learn more about autism. He is well educated and enjoys reading around other topics, but could not be persuaded to learn more about autism. He has tried to explain this to me by saying he only wanted to get to know Sasha specifically, not learn about all aspects of autism and how it might relate to other people. If I hadn't researched in the way I did, we probably wouldn't have found out about Pathological Demand Avoidance at all, and our lives would have been much more stressful. I was relieved when Chris did actually agree to read the main book about PDA, or at least enough of it to acknowledge that it seemed to be describing our girl exactly. I suspect, though, that he only read that book because I thrust it under his nose and wouldn't go away until he had.

Chris is right about many things in life and this can be helpful and interesting at times – how long it will take to get from A to B, the name of the first American president, how to best phrase an email, whether it is going to rain tomorrow and so on. He is also very sociable and personable. When it comes to understanding emotions and our family though, I think I have the edge. Maybe it comes down to maternal instinct, but I believe I am more understanding when it comes to both our daughters and more tolerant of their needs. I know all the details and can also see the bigger picture in terms of what effect actions will have, whereas I think at home Chris operates more in the here-and-now frame of mind.

I have been so lucky in the last few years to have been able to spend some short bursts of time away from home with friends and family, and Chris has stayed home to look after the girls (but please do not worry about him, he has had time away himself too!). These breaks have been much welcome respite from the ongoing daily stress of having a child permanently at home rather than in school. I think people underestimate how much of a toll that can take, not just physically in terms of trying to follow up with emails and calls and sorting legal documents, pushing for any kind of support, but also mentally in terms of trying to encourage action and development for your child whilst trying to avoid a mental health crisis.

Chris understandably wants to do things his way in terms of parenting when I am away, and I know he feels like I should just let him get on with it and not make comments about how I would do it differently. He is well able to look after Sasha and I am thankful for that. But he often doesn't pay attention to the little things, the things that matter to Sasha. The way that she likes her sandwiches spread with just the right amount of cheese, then cut and placed on the plate in the same way every day, the water bottles that she prefers using, the fact that she does not like to be interrupted if she is mid-flow, running around her room. His view, and that of many I imagine, would be that if we did the sandwiches differently every time for example, she would just have to get used to that and it would not be a problem most of the time. Sasha does still eat the sandwiches when he makes them because she is hungry and her diet is so limited, but that does not mean she is happy with his way of doing it. It could be said that, over time, those little things not being done 'right' for Sasha have built up so that she is far happier if it is me who does them, which in turn places an extra strain on me. And I think the part that Chris possibly doesn't see is how much more Sasha needs me once I get back from being away. There is an after-effect, a consequence of me not being there for her and things not happening the way Sasha needs them to.

Am I wrong for having made the sandwiches the same way every time over the years? Or was I right for making Sasha more comfortable every day? Would Chris have a better relationship with Sasha now if he had always spread the sandwiches the right way?! These kinds of questions go through my head on a regular basis but I have found I need to push them to the back of my mind. The sandwiches are of course just one tiny example in the grand scheme of things; there are many 'little things' like this that make up the life of our PDAer. The 'what ifs' don't help the future; there is no point wondering now what would have happened if we had done things differently. What I do know is that we didn't choose to live life like this; it would have been far easier to parent Sasha in the same way we did Tamsin, but it was Sasha's intense reactions from a very early age that made that impossible. We tried; it didn't work. As Chris said himself, during the educational Tribunal for Sasha, it would be a sign of madness to keep on trying methods that you know have failed over and over again.

I have always had a steely determination to do what I feel is right for both our girls, and although I am in no way perfect, I do not believe I have got the way I support Sasha wrong, on the whole. I am grateful that Chris has supported me with this, and not reacted in the way he might have naturally preferred to. Chris is a great father and it has made me sad at times when I have seen how Sasha treats him. She will get annoyed with him, and shout at him to leave her room as soon as he opens the door. She can say hurtful things to him at times, in a matter-of-fact way. She can be like this with all of us at times though; she is going through a stage where she insists that she does not care for any of her family, despite them all being very loving and understanding of her ways. She had great relationships with them all when she was younger, but it seemed as if, once she became a teenager, she decided that nobody could possibly understand her. I think the fact that she doesn't love herself also plays a part; she has called herself weird and commented on how she is not like the majority of teenagers. Recently she has asked me, in a very matter of fact manner, 'What's the point in me?' That is a question no parent wants to hear.

Of course, I try to talk to her about all of this during calmer times, about her feelings for herself and about family relationships, but Sasha is not a fan of conversations, especially when they are difficult. She is resolute about the idea that her feelings are valid, even though she admits there is no reason to not care about her dad or others. I know she does love Chris, although currently she would be likely to deny that if asked. They have had a relationship built on fun and jokes over the years, but this has dwindled to them having little interaction now she is a teenager. I feel for him; I also understand how much he would like to be having a typical family life, with all the usual ups and downs and goings-on. I am possibly more pragmatic than him about 'teenager' being a stage of life that comes to all children when increased hormone levels are involved, so there is no point in trying to force more contact. But I am also concerned that if we can't repair this relationship now, the future could be even more challenging. Worry gets us nowhere though and all I can do is try to take small steps as and when I see opportunities, which describes pretty much all of my life since having a PDA child.

I think it is right to recognize that living with a child who needs extra support has tested our marriage at times. That is in no way suggesting that it has been Sasha's fault, rather acknowledging that the way we have reacted, differently at times, has had an effect. I know that Chris has not always agreed with my way of doing things, and vice versa. I am sure that happens in every relationship, but in our family where the way of doing things can make or break a situation, the stakes and the stress levels are higher. He doesn't always understand why I might, or might not, want to try a specific way of approaching Sasha and at times he will not have considered or understood why it is not a good idea to go somewhere without all the planning. But on balance, I think we are a good team and have given our girls the best life they could have. I appreciate his support; I know this kind of stress and a difference in opinion over how to parent, or discipline, a child can break relationships and I have heard this happen to many in the PDA community.

Chris is not a big user of social media and neither are many of my friends; one reason for that is the age bracket we fall into. I also wonder if it might be a male versus female thing too; from insights provided by Facebook I can see that 98 per cent of my readers are female. Although I know there are pros and cons to social media, I have learnt so much from all the groups and articles that are available online, and all of that knowledge has contributed to managing our daily lives more successfully. I always suspected that the chapter Chris was writing would be the star of the show when it came to this book. Having read his chapter once I had finished writing all of mine, I think I am probably right. It is rare to hear a father's viewpoint, especially when it comes to the emotional aspects of life. My guess is that many other fathers of PDA children will have had some of the thoughts and experiences that Chris has shared, and I hope, even if they won't read the whole book, that they will read his words in the following chapter and relate.

ADVICE FOR PARENTS AND CARERS

- Bear in mind that sibling relationships do not always run smoothly in every family, regardless of additional needs. Managing relationships between PDA children and their siblings can add an extra layer of complexity though. One approach I would definitely advocate is trying to give each child quality time somehow, separate from one another. I appreciate this is more difficult for some, especially for single parents, but it is worth trying to enlist the help of family, friends, school staff or even neighbours to carve out that space or time, even if it is not for very long. Other ways of supporting siblings might include writing notes of support or recognition of their help in certain situations.

- Finding a trusted person for siblings to talk to about their own worries or struggles is a good idea, especially as some children may hold this in so as not to overload parents who they realize are already stressed.

- Consider whether activities, from shopping to holidays, really do need to be done as a family. Sometimes the resulting meltdowns will negate any of the positive aspects.

- There are plenty of resources that can help siblings to understand PDA too, from books to fact sheets to YouTube videos. Links to these can be found on the PDA Society website.

Chapter 9
LIFE AS A DUD: A FATHER'S PERSPECTIVE

London. A beautiful sunny day in the Spring of 2009. Steph, the two girls and I have gone to watch the London Marathon to see a couple of friends who are taking part. We have positioned ourselves on the Victoria Embankment, outside Portcullis House, a little to the north of Westminster Bridge. There are thousands of people – cheering on the runners, calling out to friends, enjoying the weather and the occasion. Steph and Tamsin have found their way to the crowd barriers to watch the runners, while I look after Sasha in her buggy.

Sasha decides she has had enough of being in the buggy, and wants to get out. She can't tell me this verbally – she's not yet two and her speech is yet to develop – but I know. I undo the straps and she steps out onto the pavement of the closed road. It is busy with people jostling to find a space where they can catch a glimpse of the runners. Many others are walking around, chatting to friends, heading for the tube, or a café, or the pub. Suddenly she's off, toddling amongst the crowd. Being the observant, responsible, yet slightly adventurous Dad that I am, I follow her but decide to hang back a few metres to see how far she will go before looking out for me.

About 15 minutes later, Sasha has reached Embankment tube

station having weaved her way in and out of the thronging crowds. Not once has she stopped or looked round, but does now. She turns round, looks up at me with a face that says 'what are you doing here?', and walks straight past me back towards Westminster. Another 15 minutes later and we are back outside Portcullis House. Aged 22 months, she has just walked the best part of a mile, independently, amongst a crowd of thousands, and got back to where she started without any input from an adult, and seemingly without a care in the world.

I realize right there and then that Sasha is different.

* * *

About a year later, Steph, Sasha and I are in the office of a consultant paediatrician. Sasha and Steph have been here before to find out why her speech is delayed. We already know it isn't because of a hearing impairment, as we first thought. On the last visit the paediatrician mentioned that Sasha might have autism, which I took to mean it was one of many possibilities.

This time she asks: 'Have you thought any more about a diagnosis of autism?', which I find slightly odd. We say yes, but wondered what else it could be. 'Oh, it's definitely autism,' she says, unequivocally; she must have known last time. I can see Steph welling up. I don't know what to think – I don't even know what autism is, really, other than a condition where some kids and a few adults act a bit strange and have obsessive interests. But that is that – we walked into the paediatrician's office with a typical two-year-old, and leave with an autistic child. Once we get home, Steph and I talk about it for a few minutes. Steph has, of course, been reading up on autism and explains to me what it could mean; I know immediately that our lives are changed forever. I can't stop myself from crying: partly because of the unknown, and partly, shamefully, because I know that this will restrict my life and I won't be able to do many of the things I want to do. Pure selfishness.

So, the journey begins, but there's no map (I love a map!), and if I'm honest I don't know where the destination is, or even if there is a destination. We tell friends and family, all of whom are unswervingly supportive with offers of help and sometimes advice. Many of them give us encouragement with a variation of 'our little Johnny has a friend at school who is autistic, he's a lovely little boy and all his classmates love him'. More than a few friends tell us of autistic family members, which we didn't know about previously. I wonder why we didn't know – were we not paying attention, or did they not tell us?

We then start the process of what seems to be endless appointments with various services: more time with the paediatrician, Children's Mental Health, the local Autism Advisory service, courses run by charities, and so on. I go to as many of these as possible, but sometimes work gets in the way. At a paediatrician appointment we are asked if there is autism in the family. I mention a couple of my relatives who are, let's just say, very clever but a little particular about most things in life. And then I think about me – how I was terribly fussy about food until my late teens when I discovered beer, or how I have a memory that can remember the most obscure things.

Oh my God, this is my fault!

It's not long before I realize that no-one is at fault, and indeed being autistic isn't something that can be described as a 'fault' – it is simply a brain that processes information in a different way to what is considered to be the norm. Or perhaps autistic people are the typical ones?

Through the support groups and courses, we meet dozens of other parents with children recently diagnosed as autistic. Some seem ashamed, or even in denial, that their child is autistic. I hear one dad say that he's only there because his wife insisted he came along, and that his daughter is 'just a bit quirky'. Some parents have not told anyone, and I am really surprised, which often surprises them. Personally, I just don't get this – I live by the principle that if you tell enough people about challenges in your life then you will always find someone who can help and support. As it turns out, we have found many, many wonderful people who have provided support and care, sometimes without realizing it.

What strikes me in these sessions is how different each child is, how many have other diagnoses (ADHD and OCD being particularly prevalent), and how all the parents are desperate for answers and advice to help them with their child. The bad news is that often there aren't answers, simply because every child is unique in their own way. The good news is that because of that uniqueness there is often no right or wrong; it is up to the parents to determine – discover – what works best for their child.

Steph throws herself into this new world of ours, buys several books on autism and busies herself making contacts: parents, specialists, teachers; she wants to learn about the subject so that she can help Sasha as much as possible. Over time this would cause some friction between us: particularly in the early days she would want to tell me about what she had found out, people she had spoken to, things I should read or do relating to autism. I was just not interested (and generally I'm still not, sorry), and this frustrates her. It's not that I don't care, far from it, but my brain just doesn't work like that. This might sound heartless, but I care about Sasha, not autism. That's not to say I don't know about the subject now – after 13 years plenty of information has sunk in. But I need to process this, and cope with it, in the way that I find the easiest.

While I didn't really know what autism was, I did have an idea. The first time I knowingly began to understand the condition was when watching the third series of the TV drama *Waterloo Road* (coincidentally first broadcast a few months after Sasha was born), the first episode of which featured a girl with Asperger Syndrome. This explained in very broad terms what the condition was, and it was a revelation for me; I realized then that it was not an illness or a 'phase' that some people go through, but a condition for life, and that Asperger's was a form of autism – I had no idea there were different flavours! It also made me realize that a colleague at work who had a history of difficulty with professional relationships almost certainly had undiagnosed autism of some kind; I further suspected there were many more people I knew with the condition, although at that time I didn't realize how close to me they would be.

I don't remember when PDA (Pathological Demand Avoidance) was first mentioned, but it must have been that Steph had been doing some research and found the details. When she shows me, I am in no doubt; that is 100 per cent Sasha. It's a revelation and a relief; she has something that other people have, now we can work with it, learn from the experience of others, and take the steps the medical and mental health professions suggest. Little did I know how wrong I was. But there's another thing – in one small respect, PDA is also me: my fussy eating, although much better now, is still with me and will be forever. It's not that I don't want to eat all those other foods in the supermarket, or the other lovely looking dishes on the menu – I just can't. I physically can't put them in my mouth, it fills me with horror about how they may taste or what the texture is if I don't know in advance. For Sasha it is the same with almost all aspects of her life. She wants to do things, but just can't; this is how I relate to her life.

As we move through life – nursery, then on to school, after school activities, clubs and so on – we meet more families, new friends and other people who come into contact with Sasha. We make a point of telling them what to expect, how to manage her, and that we are always available for help and advice. Curiously, it is the professionals who seem to be the least receptive, or perhaps it is understandable, as they will have been trained for this (or so I assume) and I often get the impression that we are considered as worried parents who don't realize that the professionals deal with this sort of thing all the time. Almost without exception, the professionals either come back to ask for help (good), or make mistakes and try to carry on regardless (bad), resulting in Sasha invariably giving up on those activities.

Other parents, though, are much more interested. Back in the days when Sasha was invited to playdates and parties, parents were very understanding, and would be particularly accommodating in providing the right environment, the right food, and being ready to ask us for help. I'm sure Sasha appreciated this (probably without realizing it), and I know Steph and I did. If you are reading – thank you – you know who you are.

In those first few years the difference between Sasha and her peers was not so obvious. That's not to say we had it easy – there were several bumps in the road. One occasion I shall never forget, when Sasha was aged four. I had taken both girls to the supermarket one Saturday evening to do the weekly shop, which, if we took it slowly and subsequently visited McDonalds (I hope this wasn't the start of the habit), meant Steph could have two or three hours to herself at home. I remember at the time her saying I was brave taking them both out, and so it proved. The shopping went well, with both girls helping to find items on the shelves and predictably at least one of them becoming temporarily 'lost'. All good fun. However, when we reached the checkouts a switch flipped in Sasha, and she was suddenly quite distressed. I have no idea why – perhaps the noise of the checkout 'beeps', or that it was busier there, or perhaps that we had to wait a while in line for the checkout. She was upset, and wanted to be picked up and held. You might think this is easy. I challenge any grown adult to attempt unloading a trolley-full of wine shopping on to the belt with one hand whilst simultaneously carrying and comforting a 95th percentile-sized child with the other arm and keeping an eye out for your second child, a curious six-year-old with a propensity to wander off in the blink of an eye. And because I am always over-concerned about what other people think, also carrying off a conversation with the lady on the checkout about the weather, how wonderful the girls are, the price of fish, etc. I'm pleased to say I managed it, and felt rather proud of myself, if a little sore in the arm.

Then I realized I had to pack the shopping into the bags. Of course, being a young, able, British man, I naturally refuse assistance. Let me tell you that it is not possible to pack shopping into bags with one free hand whilst carrying a child in the other. So, I had to put Sasha down. Whilst I knew what was coming, I think it was quite a surprise to everyone else in the supermarket – a massive meltdown. Sasha lay down on the floor, face up, turned up the volume to 11 and wailed. I still don't know what I did to calm her down, but I think after about a minute I picked her up again, found a seat nearby, plonked her on there and mentioned the imminent trip to McDonalds. I'm sure that Tamsin helped on that occasion by talking to her gently, and I now hold the record for packing shopping in the London Colney branch of Sainsbury's. From that day on, if I ever see a parent with an upset child trying to pack shopping at the checkout, I always offer to help with an understanding mention of 'I've been there, don't worry'. Rarely is the offer refused; the relief is palpable – sometimes it seems that it is the best thing that has *ever* happened to them.

In those early years we realized how Sasha reacts badly to being told that she has done something wrong, or even that she could do something better. Often she will curl up into a ball – we call it 'mushrooming' – throw a blanket or duvet over herself and scream if anyone tries to talk to her. We learned that in some cases this doesn't stop her from doing things she knows are wrong, and also, worse, it stops her from trying to discover as she is anxious about getting it wrong. After several years I have learned how to manage situations like this now, and try to use humour wherever possible, usually by pretending to be stupid. She rarely screams and shouts now, but when she is upset she now withdraws completely and will be found in her room sobbing gently, which is absolutely heart-breaking. Not so much because of the emotion, but because Sasha now realizes that she can't do certain things, and is more upset with herself than upset with us.

To help with writing this chapter I have looked through some old photos. We have many of course, probably too many of me to be honest, as Steph is much better than me at taking pictures to capture the moments. However, there are a few that I managed to take when Steph was away for more than a day or two when she was visiting friends, family or on a well-deserved short holiday. These are of Sasha and me having great fun: in the garden, on a couple of walks, in the paddling pool or hot tub. At these times Sasha switches her reliance and need for interaction to me, and I effectively become substitute 'mum'; I'm in no doubt that I am second choice parent but it is wonderful all the same, and I cherish those times, and these few photos are precious to me. However – and this is difficult – Steph never sees Sasha behave like this to me because, obviously, she is away. Steph thus finds it difficult to switch off duty, 'let go' if you like, and is anxious that I will upset Sasha by doing the wrong thing. I will get various texts or calls making sure I have done what Sasha wants at the right time in the right order. Sometimes Sasha will text Steph when she is away to tell her that something or other is not quite right. Naturally this worries Steph, who will then call me, and I'm often oblivious to whatever the issue is. But – and this is important – Sasha is invariably fine, and there is no need for Steph to worry. And, if I do mess up, then it is up to me to resolve. But it very rarely happens.

One of the unexpectedly nice things about having Sasha is that friends or colleagues are always interested in how she is getting on, and how we are getting on with her. As I said earlier, I'm not one to hide things and I will tell all, perhaps maybe too much; if so 'sorry, I'm not sorry', as talking about it helps me greatly. Many will listen, pause a little while and then say 'it must be difficult', or 'I don't know how you cope'. The stock answer is, naturally, that we don't know any different, this is us and the cards we have been dealt, and we just have to get on with it. Sure, it is difficult sometimes, and we can't do many things we want to do, but we have met many, many more families who have far bigger challenges than us. So, I say to my friends: 'No matter how bad you feel, remember there is always someone, somewhere, having a tougher time.'

Reflecting on the past 12 years, I can now see a gradual regression in Sasha in many areas of her life. This is not easy to observe when you are with your child every day, week after week, year after year: you miss the little changes. But then, as I have mentioned earlier, I have a great memory and I can remember when she happily ate Weetabix, cheese and bananas, loved coming out for a walk around the park, and would happily engage with her grandparents. I can remember taking Sasha and Tamsin, on my own, on a day trip to Leeds by train for a family event about seven years ago. All of that, and more, has stopped; indeed it is unthinkable now. I'm not afraid to say that I'm scared to the bottom of my soul about what else Sasha might stop doing, or eating, and where this will all end.

For the last few years my relationship with Sasha has felt more like adult to adult than parent to child. She is quite candid that she loves her Mum, and to a lesser extent her sister; but towards me, it's a begrudging acceptance that I'm her Dad and that I understand

and help her more than most other people. About four years ago, whether by accident or design, Sasha started to refer to me as her 'Dud' rather than Dad. I still don't know if she realizes that the word 'dud' is, by one definition, 'a thing that fails to work properly, or is otherwise unsatisfactory or worthless'. I expect she does know, and it is a private joke of her own; her sense of humour is brilliant, if somewhat acidic and sarcastic.

We have some occasional laughs but almost exclusively at my expense; if I stub my toe, or trip up, or bang my head for example, she can't help laughing. I play up to this of course, and also pretend to forget things or be generally stupid. She quite enjoys calling me an 'idiot' when I do these things, and I know that most of the time she is joking, but occasionally she will say it out of context or with a harsh tone to her voice and that hurts me. I have learned to be careful in how I react in these situations; previously I would be cross with her and she would immediately become very upset, because she doesn't understand why saying the same thing in a different context can mean a different thing. Now I let it wash over, and perhaps make fun of it. I know where I stand in the family hierarchy.

Perhaps what is most frustrating is thinking about how we might have done some things differently. I know that if it was entirely up to me we would have had quite a different approach to many aspects of Sasha's life. Would she have been different? Would our lives be easier? This is absolutely not to relieve myself of any responsibility, or blame Steph for how things have turned out; quite the opposite, I think Steph is a terrific mum who has been, without doubt, a better parent than I have been in bringing up the girls. Of course, we will never know if, or how, our lives would have been different, and it is more than likely that our lives could have turned out to be much, much worse had I been calling the shots. Nevertheless, I often have dreams where Sasha is chatting to us like a well-adjusted teenager and living a regular life, and I wonder what we could have done differently to achieve that. I feel a deep sense of guilt for letting Steph deal with all the administrative burden of Sasha's life, particularly the educational side, and I wonder if I could have made a difference had I spent more time helping on this. Steph and I have had a number of disagreements during our dealings with the educational service; Steph is entirely focused on what she thinks is best for Sasha, whilst I try to look at it from various perspectives, including what the professionals and the Local Authority will be thinking. But deep down I know that Steph has been right almost all the time, and that the educational service has been under-resourced and in some cases simply not capable of understanding what Sasha needs, but it doesn't stop me thinking about what might have been.

But what might have been? I am a Governor at a local secondary school, and spend a few hours a month there for meetings, conducting visits and talking to the staff and students. Recently I attended an assembly for Year 10, part of which was a brilliant presentation by six of the students to the rest of the year on personal image, bullying and the emotional rollercoaster that teenagers can go through. One of the students was at primary school with Sasha, and then it hit me again: here were a couple of hundred young adults all of Sasha's age, being readied to go into further education, the world of work, and adult life. I so desperately want Sasha to be like them: independent, to be able to look after herself, buy and prepare food, travel unaccompanied, perhaps get a job and live away from home. That seems a remote prospect now, more remote than it did five years ago. Life is unfair Chris, deal with it. But on the other side of the coin, Sasha isn't getting herself into trouble, or being bullied (nor being a bully), or spending money on useless tat, or going to parties and getting drunk or involved in drugs. So, I suppose I don't have that to worry about, take the positives!

Aside from our wonderful daughter, the best thing about having a child with additional needs is how it has opened my eyes to the wider world of disability and mental health. In my view, the understanding of autism and other less visible mental health conditions has improved dramatically over the past ten years or so, and this is to the great credit of those who champion these causes. Not least, Steph, who has made a real difference in this field; I'm so proud of her and how she has gone about helping others understand the world of autism, PDA and mental health. Above all, I admire how she has 'kept the show on the road' and held her head high through everything we have been through, as she bears most of the burden. More than anything, I hope that the key message Steph tries to give is heard more widely in future: some people are just different, and that's ok.

I will leave you with my top ten tips to being a Dad (or Dud) of an autistic/PDA child:

1. Your child, your rules.

2. Let people know. Most will understand, many will help.

3. Accept that your future will change, indeed it already has. But it can be better if you choose to make it so.

4. Every autistic child is different. You will learn what works. It may take time, and the ride may be bumpy.

5. Take as much advice as you want, but don't be afraid, and refer to Rule 1.

6. Your partner and/or other people involved may, no, *will*, see things differently. That's ok – if everyone thought the same life would be dull.

7. Siblings can help, particularly in the younger years, but don't grow to rely on them – in time they will have their own lives to lead.

8. Remember there are others in the family who need love and attention too, and that includes you. Look after yourself; if you sink so will your child.

9. Sometimes, life is unfair. So what? Play the hand you have been dealt.

10. There are many others in a similar position as you. Some have had it easier; some tougher. You are not the first to do this, and you *can* do it too.

Chapter 10

DEALING WITH OTHER PEOPLE

Even before the autism diagnosis we could see that Sasha's reactions to everyday events were different to her older sister's. Initially we had tried to parent our girls in the same way, using the same traditional parenting approaches that I think many people expect to use when they have children. These simply did not work for Sasha, which is why we had to alter our parenting style. I am not sure that it has crossed Chris' mind much, but I have spent a lot of time feeling that this has led to my parenting being criticized behind my back.

On the same day that the introductory session was held at Sasha's new nursery, there was a talk at the school for all parents of Tamsin's year group. That meant that Sasha had to attend the talk with me, directly after her nursery session. Around 40 parents were quietly sitting in a small classroom, listening to information about the maths curriculum. That could have been called 'a recipe for disaster' in our family book, and it was the kind of situation I might usually have tried to avoid because I knew it would be difficult for Sasha. That particular day though, I must have been feeling brave, so we gave it a go. Sasha was very well behaved, thanks to a bit of distraction from a colouring program on the school computer, followed by chocolate buttons for a snack, and I then allowed her to play with my iPhone. However, this caused a problem when we realized it was not possible to have the volume switched on in this group situation. Lots of her favourite games at that point involved music. She asked me repeatedly to 'fix it' (i.e. switch the sound on), but when I did not, she began to get agitated and asked repeatedly to go home, her voice becoming louder with each request. She seemed to have no awareness that everyone else in the room was quiet, listening to the teacher's talk. That might be how lots of toddlers would react, but by the age of four, as Sasha was then, children were generally expected to know when they should be quiet in a situation like this. As the session was nearing its end anyway, I agreed to take her home early, to avoid the otherwise inevitable meltdown. I slipped out as quietly as I could, but as I left I assumed that other mums would think I was 'pandering' to her and that she was a spoiled child, getting her own way.

That was one of the most difficult aspects of parenting Sasha: having to accept that others would form their own opinions of my parenting without having the full facts. No one else knew her like I did though, and for me it became almost second nature to know when to push the boundaries and make her do something she wasn't keen on or when to try to avoid that meltdown. That day, if I had insisted we stay longer, she would have had a meltdown in that classroom, and I knew that no one else would have been able to hear a word the teacher said from that point on. The flipside of me managing the behaviour and leaving early in these kinds of situations was that few people understood what the outcome might be, because I would rarely let them see Sasha get to that point of meltdown. It felt too difficult to describe how it was not just her being naughty and then having a tantrum because she wanted her own way. There was more to it than that; Sasha seemed not to understand why it wasn't possible to do things her way, or to do them as soon as she wanted.

When Sasha was a toddler, I had to gradually admit defeat in terms of attending organized sessions, because they clearly didn't suit her. I began to feel isolated; I was unable to socialize, even though I desperately wanted to. When it came to school life, I would have loved to throw myself into volunteering for every fair, trip and cake sale, but after a while I realized that trying to do any of this with Sasha in tow was impossible. She was not able to amuse herself easily and she always needed my full attention. Sasha didn't react well to strangers or people who didn't understand her needs, so we weren't able to find babysitters easily, a situation that lasted until her teenage years.

I remember another mum with slightly younger children than mine telling me one day that she felt I talked to Sasha as though she was younger than her actual age. That mum was quite surprised when I explained that I needed to keep my language simple because Sasha would not otherwise understand whatever the issue was at the time. It was something that her own children, and Tamsin at a younger age, would have automatically understood without any need for a big explanation. I knew that the lack of understanding was difficult for others to grasp because in many ways Sasha seemed so bright and capable, as if she was at the same level as her peers. Over time we realized this was known as a spiky profile – meaning there were strengths in some areas, but skills lacking in others. Sasha's true ability has always been difficult to determine, and this has contributed to her being referred to as a 'complex' child.

I sometimes wonder if I am referred to as a 'complex' parent? Or if others think that I worry unnecessarily, that I pay too much attention to the little things? I wouldn't describe myself as an anxious person. I would consider myself calm and rational, and I hope people who have known me well both before and after having children would agree. When our eldest was a toddler it did not cross my mind that other people might judge me, but within the first couple of years of Sasha's life those thoughts often swirled around my mind. When Sasha attended the specialist nursery (TRACKS), it was such a relief to meet other parents and staff members who automatically understood autistic behaviour. Sasha no longer stood out as being the one who was different, and neither did I.

When the girls were young we would regularly visit a local activity farm, a big attraction with farmyard animals, funfair rides, outdoor assault courses, tractor rides and indoor soft play. Up until Sasha was around the age of eight, we would visit this farm at least once a week. Sasha was very happy there most of the time, having fun with her sister in a place that had become familiar. When the weather was wet, we would end up indoors in the busy soft play area. There were three sections to the soft play: one for babies to 18 months, one for 18 months to five years old and a much bigger section for the older children. For a long time, Sasha preferred to be in the section that was deemed too young for her. She kept asking for the baby soft play area until around the age of three. I felt bad about breaking the rules by letting her in there. I would always be on edge, waiting for parents of younger children to challenge me, especially as Sasha was not a small child and was obviously too old for the area. She wasn't particularly boisterous though and would spend a long time enjoying the machines that blew plastic balls up in the air. Or she would climb carefully up the small soft slide, crawl through under-neath it with a big smile, or collect the balls, happy in her own little world, with her own self-directed missions. It was difficult having to stop her from entering the baby area but at some point it definitely felt like we were outstaying our welcome. We explained to Sasha that she would need to start playing in the middle area provided for slightly older children, and I think the only reason she agreed to that was because her older sister persuaded her to. Tamsin was by then almost too old to be in the middle area herself and would rather have moved up to the bigger section, but I think she kindly agreed to take Sasha in because she instinctively understood the challenge posed by Sasha being in the baby area.

From around the age of seven, Sasha moved up into the play area for the oldest children. Tamsin was already enjoying this independently, but I would have to follow Sasha around, over and under every obstacle, because leaving her alone could lead to issues. I hadn't needed to do that for Tamsin. I remember feeling very nervous the first time Sasha asked to go into this soft play area on her own, without Tamsin, leaving me sitting at a table in the big area with all the other parents. Sasha didn't return for a long while, so I knew I would need to go and search for her. I made my way through the soft play area calling her name. I found her in a mushroom position, kneeling down on the mats with her hands over her ears. She couldn't tell me what was wrong, but my guess was that some other children had tried to talk to her, or tried to tell her she was not allowed to do something, or else it might have been that the noise and crowding was simply too overwhelming.

Of course, lots of parents might experience missing children in soft play areas, or children who would come back to them crying. Others might have children who react violently when challenged or overwhelmed. But Sasha's reactions always seem so much more extreme than those of other children. She would not lash out physically but her mushroom position would last a long time and she would be unable to talk, other than to scream 'go away'.

The times we had used the Queue Assist pass at the theme park, I was very aware of the challenging looks from other parents with children younger than mine. To an outsider, Sasha didn't appear any different to other children, and her inability to wait in a queue might have come across as a spoiled brat temper tantrum. Their children might have been whingey because they didn't enjoy queueing either, but the difference was that most of them could manage queueing, they just didn't like it. Our older daughter had always been perfectly capable of waiting in queues; it wasn't that I had not tried hard enough to teach Sasha how to be patient. Although I knew that Sasha needed the accommodations, I could see that other people didn't understand why. It was impossible to explain to others in this type of situation though. It was always difficult going out to places like these, but in my mind I weighed up the challenging times with the fun that was also had, and I remained determined to get out of the house as much as possible.

When it came to education settings, I was sometimes made to feel like I was too involved or was giving too much detail about our daughter. There were also occasions when I felt not listened to, especially during some of the EHCP review meetings and when there have been difficulties attending school. This eventually led to me making a conscious effort to arrange meetings for when Sasha's dad was available too. My experience has been that his voice seemed to hold more importance when it came to meetings about our child. I will admit to finding this both bizarre and frustrating, given that I, as the person who spent the most time with Sasha, was likely to understand her needs best. For several years my name appeared at the top of Sasha's EHCP paperwork, as the main carer and main contact. But then inexplicably, after one particular EHCP review, the paperwork returned with Sasha's dad's name at the top. The EHCP was the same format as it had always been, but this time our names had been purposefully transposed. I have no idea why and maybe I should give the benefit of the doubt and say it was some sort of admin error, but it certainly felt very deliberate. There are many times that parents of children with SEND are made to feel like they are the problem. What I would have appreciated along the way was some kind of acknowledgement that it was the school environments and the education system that were at fault, rather than the insinuation that it was me or my daughter causing the issues.

Oppositional is a word that the paediatrician attributed to our daughter at an early age. Oppositional Defiant Disorder (ODD) is a diagnosis sometimes given to children who are not behaving in what society classes as a typical manner. In order to receive a diagnosis of ODD, children would typically be described as defiant, disobedient, malicious and provocative. They are seen as having emotional and behavioural difficulties, or conduct problems. They may have experienced difficult social environments and use behaviour as a means of attention, a way of expressing their anger or to hide their low self-esteem. It is said that children with ODD tend to be less keen on embarrassing themselves in front of their peers. PDA children, on the other hand, may be more likely to have unpredictable outbursts, even in front of their peers, and they often try to control all social interaction without understanding why their peers do not like it. The latest revisions of the medical manuals recognize that children with an ODD diagnosis would not be showing characteristics of autism, but this could be problematic for clinicians when we consider how many autistic individuals spend a lot of time trying to mask their true selves in order to fit in with others and may mean that PDA children are misdiagnosed as having ODD, which is problematic as the strategies and approaches which help are quite different (see Chapter 11). Parents know their children best however, and I think many would notice the indicators for autism, whereas some clinicians in a short appointment may not; this links back to my earlier suggestion of keeping a diary and evidence of how your child reacts in everyday situations.

Children with ODD are described as having long-lasting, aggressive and defiant behaviours that are extreme, and whilst I understand this may appear to apply to some PDA children, it was not, and is not, a good description of our daughter. Attachment disorder (or any kind of trauma) is also not relevant to our family situation.

The following comments, and more along the same lines, have been made to many parents of PDA children, including me:

'PDA is just a name for children who don't want to do as they are told.'

'PDA doesn't exist, it's just lazy parenting.'

'Your child isn't autistic; they just need firm boundaries.'

'You need to be more strict.'

'She's had too much chance to pick and choose what she wants to do.'

'You should just say no to her.'

'Rules and routine will help.'

'If she doesn't learn how to do that now, what will she do when she's an adult?'

I think there might be a tendency to judge parents of PDA children as being lazy and inept at parenting. One of the most difficult issues about Pathological Demand Avoidance for others to understand is the fact that there are times when some demands will be complied with. So, if these PDA children can do it once, why not the other times? They are not avoiding *all* demands... doesn't that mean they are picking and choosing? For certain periods in the last few years Sasha has gone to school, and worn a uniform, and brushed her teeth. Surely they are all demands which she has complied with? They are, but it was pointless to assume 'well if she can do that, you can make her do anything' or that because she had done it once she would do it again. There are so many factors that affect what is possible, every single day.

Even when we had recognized her needs and were being as flexible as possible in the way we parented Sasha, we found that she might be able to manage to comply with demands one day, but not the next. For individuals with other profiles of autism, routine is often favoured, and in many cases, routine is actually vital to get through each day. Knowing what is going to happen helps lessen the anxiety for some children. We knew that routine helped Sasha in some ways, but the Pathological Demand Avoidance would override that. She couldn't cope with being told what to do every day, she needed to be in control. So, we experienced a constant see-saw of trying to have a routine but that routine being constantly interrupted or changed. Novelty and finding something new to try were welcomed by Sasha, as long as she had suggested them.

Other people outside of the home do not see the amount of effort that goes into making any little changes in the daily routine. I wish that I could invite all of the judgemental people who make those kinds of disparaging comments to come and live with us. That might help them understand what it is that makes our younger girl different from our older girl. We see and live the difference every day. I do feel lucky in some way that Sasha was our second child, because I was able to compare her reactions to those of her older sister and see the difference. We are also lucky that Sasha acted the same way in school and other environments as she did for us at home. She hasn't masked on the whole, something which many other autistic girls and some boys seem to use as their coping mechanism. Many

PDA children do have the added fear of breaking the rules, so they will try their hardest to conform at school all day. Sadly, the effect this has is similar to a pressure cooker; when they are home again, where they feel comfortable, they are more likely to explode at even the smallest demand.

All autistic people are unique individuals, with different personalities and differing needs. Overlying indicators or common characteristics of autism (or any condition) need to exist in order for it to be a diagnosable condition or difference, but those descriptors will relate to individuals to different degrees. Descriptions of the diagnosable attributes of PDA have already evolved over the 12 years since our daughter received her diagnosis. This happens because understanding improves as more autistic adults and families share their experiences, and because research into what autism means and how autistic people can be best supported is undertaken regularly. Research papers around PDA do exist and can be found online, and research is ongoing.

Some people have told me they don't believe in labels for children, but I view a diagnosis as a signpost rather than as a label. In my opinion, giving more detail about individuals should happen as a matter of course. The overarching autism diagnosis does not do much to help others to understand an individual's specific needs, and assumptions can be wrongly made from such a general signpost. Some friends have tried to explain how they feel that grouping individuals together with one label can be detrimental, because people will then make assumptions about what their needs are without actually getting to know the individual, and I can understand their viewpoint to some extent. There does seem to be some stigma attached to the term PDA, in terms of it often being linked to explosive or aggressive behaviour, something that our girl does not exhibit. There have been times when I have worried that having

PDA specified in Sasha's EHCP is a bad idea. As noted earlier, I suspect at least one school refused to consider her for that very reason, having not even met her in person. There would have been no point in us not giving a full description of Sasha to any school though, given how much we knew different approaches could make or break situations. So even if we had left the term PDA off the paperwork, the anxiety and demand avoidance would still have been evident.

Would I mind if research decided at some point in the future that PDA was not 'a thing'? I will be watching with interest for future research publications on the topic, but I can honestly say I do not mind what people call this presentation of autism. I have been happy to use the term PDA to highlight the challenges in life that our younger daughter faces. Our experiences are very real; saying there is no such thing as PDA would not change any of that. Autism does not describe Sasha in enough detail, and ODD, trauma, conduct disorder or attachment disorder are not applicable in her case. Some people say they don't believe in PDA, and they don't believe that it is impossible to make children do what you want them to. All I can say in response is that they have not lived with my child. I hope some of what is written in this book gives a more detailed impression, but, of course, there are not enough pages to describe every part of her character.

Sasha is not exactly the same as all the other individuals diagnosed with PDA. I have still never met another child quite like Sasha. But being part of a community of people who all feel like the term PDA fits them or their child does bring some kind of inner peace and less isolation. Comfort is gained from knowing there are other people who understand the challenges that are created by a society that expects people to behave in certain predetermined ways. Having Sasha has definitely opened my eyes to life more than they otherwise would have been and I think the biggest change in me is that I now ask more questions – of myself and others.

ADVICE FOR PARENTS AND CARERS

- Try not to let comments from people who do not know your child impact how you feel. Remember that parents are experts when it comes to their own children; you are the people who can see the impact of demands on your child.

- Worry less about what others think. They are not living with your child 24/7 and do not have all the answers. People will always judge what they do not understand.

- In any way you can, gently educate others about what does work for your child. Remember they can't know what they don't know!

Chapter 11

WHAT WORKS FOR US

n her early research, Professor Elizabeth Newson noted that children with the PDA profile 'did not respond to educational and management approaches recommended for most individuals on the autism spectrum'.[1] Newson discovered that PDA children responded best to novelty, humour and flexibility rather than rigid structures and routines. After 15 years of living with a PDAer, I have learnt a lot about our PDA girl and how to support her, and I would definitely agree that novelty, humour and flexibility are the best approaches to take. Despite plenty of practice, there are still times when I do not get it right. Our children are constantly evolving and maturing and we need to roll with the times and adjust the approaches we try – and that is true for parenting any child. Figuring out what works for PDA children can be a different level of exhausting. Helping our children by working out what their needs are and finding suitable solutions to support them is key.

I would always suggest starting with reading more, in order to better understand PDA. The PDA Society website contains a great deal of helpful information and is always the first resource I

---

1   Elizabeth O'Nions, Judith Gould, Phil Christie, Christopher Gillberg, Essi Viding and Francesca Happé (2016) 'Identifying features of "pathological demand avoidance" using the Diagnostic Interview for Social and Communication Disorders (DISCO).' *European Child and Adolescent Psychiatry* 25, 407–419.

recommend. There have been several books published covering the topic of PDA, and online there are thousands of other sources of information, including blogs and YouTube videos, podcasts and social media posts. It is always worth remembering that our PDA children grow up to be PDA adults, so I suggest researching and digesting the experiences shared by adult PDAers, such as Julia Daunt, Riko Ryuki and Sally Cat and others, because they give many insights into being a PDAer.

Dr Ross Greene is a clinical psychologist who spent many years working with children who were labelled as challenging. His philosophy concentrates on the idea that 'kids do well if they can'. He goes on to explain that if they are not doing well, they must be missing skills that would help them do well. He urges everyone to 'change your lenses' – in other words, consider our own beliefs and our reasons for expecting certain behaviour from our children. Once we have changed our lenses, we might react differently to the child's behaviour, and look for ways to help rather than reacting with consequences or punishment, for example. It is impossible to do Dr Greene's work justice in such a small section of this book; he is author of the books *The Explosive Child*, *Lost at School*, *Lost & Found* and *Raising Human Beings*, and his website is full of helpful information.

As parents or educators of PDA children we need to assume a new role. We need to become detectives, uncovering what the issues are, and finding out what is actually causing any unwanted behaviour. At the same time, we should also change our lenses and question whether the behaviour is actually as bad as we think it is. Clearly violence and hurting others are unacceptable, but maybe when it comes to some other behaviours it could be worth rethinking why or whether they should be stopped.

Most parents learn quickly that PDA individuals are generally best supported using parenting approaches that differ from the usual ways many of us would expect to bring up children. Many children with ODD seem to benefit from more rigid boundaries and good use of reward and consequence schemes, but PDA children do not generally respond to these methods in the same way. In PDA, the avoidance of, and refusal to comply with, everyday demands is driven by high anxiety. It is not caused by an inherent desire to be oppositional and gain attention. The following ways to help are examples of how we have managed to make family life work with our PDAer – simple suggestions that run through everyday life.

Plan ahead

Having some kind of plan and structure is more likely to ensure a day or a trip out goes well. The more information you can provide about what will happen on an excursion, the better, including timing and method of travel, what can be expected once there, visuals of what the environment will be like and who will be there. All of this preparation is more likely to make an event successful, but you should also try to expect the unexpected. An example of this was when Sasha was 12 and I took her for a cycling lesson. She had always wanted to learn to ride a bike but her anxiety prevented her when she was younger. So, when I heard of an instructor locally who offered individual lessons and who has had lots of experience and success with children with additional needs, I suggested to Sasha that we might try, and I was pleased when she agreed. However, when we arrived at the venue, I realized that the instructor was an older man. I had probably subconsciously expected this, due to his level of experience, but I hadn't thought to check and so I hadn't prepared Sasha for this eventuality. As we approached him, Sasha's demeanour instantly changed and I knew she wasn't comfortable. She has difficulty accepting being taught by anyone, but in particular by older people. I don't know why, and of course I have attempted to challenge her preconceptions, but as many parents of

PDA children will understand, once their minds are made up it is difficult to persuade them otherwise. Sasha did get on the bike but only went one lap around the car park with the instructor holding onto the bike before her body language told me that she would go no further. Less understanding parents or educators might say that we gave up too easily, but my years of experience have taught me that there is no point forcing Sasha to do anything.

Managing other people's reactions to your child is also difficult to plan for. As with most things PDA, there is never any guarantee of success, even if you have done as much preparation as you thought possible. Thinking about what may happen in different scenarios and keeping your options open is important. I always do my research in advance, to make sure there is a chance to escape before it all gets too much and a meltdown happens. Make sure there is a quiet space, or easy access to an exit, and make sure your child has items that will help with sensory overload. Can they take a comfort or fiddle toy with them? Are they able to wear their own headphones and listen to music? Small adjustments can sometimes be the difference between success and failure.

Be flexible

One of the biggest challenges with PDA is having to stay on your toes daily, being ready to change tack and pull different ideas out of the bag. A phrase often used is that living with a PDAer is like 'walking on eggshells'. Although planning ahead is vital, an ability to quickly adapt to situations that are not going as well as you hoped can make all the difference. There's no point having fixed ideas of how you want to achieve something; flexibility is the key to success. That could mean flexibility in the moment when everything is starting to unravel, or thinking in advance about what you are hoping to happen. It is worth considering why you want your child to behave in a certain way. For example, if you are expecting your child to sit at a table to eat their food with you at a specific time of your choosing, can you be flexible about the time or the place?

Build a trusting relationship

As is the case for most autistic children, good, trusting relationships are crucial for progress. Trust can be built up when the child realizes that the difficulties they are facing are appreciated and understood. Even if your PDA child is a good communicator, it is essential to keep watching every little reaction they have, to unpick where the anxiety stems from and to understand what the issues are. Being proactive, in terms of figuring out solutions, will help in the long run. Successful relationships can help reduce anxiety levels.

Offer choices

Not too many choices, as otherwise the demand and pressure of picking one of those options may be too much. Maybe let your child choose where they want to go from a short list. Having different options on the start time for an activity will be much better received than an instruction involving the word 'now'. When children are younger, it may be possible to get away with offering a choice which you would like to see as the outcome versus another not-so-appealing option. Beware though, because PDA children are often wise to attempts at 'tricking' in terms of coming to a solution that suits you best, and this can lead to a breakdown in trust.

Choose words carefully

The choice of language is so important when it comes to PDA individuals. Even when our girl was still quite young and not properly speaking, I would joke with people that her favourite word was no, but only if she was the one using it. If we dared to use no, it would pretty much guarantee an outburst of extreme anxiety as control was lost, and nothing else would be achieved that day. It is important to explain that this was not the same as a toddler tantrum (or a teenage tantrum for that matter). Was Sasha capable of having a simple tantrum over being told no? Yes, she was, and the difference between tantrum and meltdown took some working out initially. Over time though, we began to understand when the upset was driven by anxiety and a need to avoid demands rather than a want, a material wish for something that she couldn't have. Of course, there are some occasions when it is necessary to use the word no, and a good example is when there may be danger involved. I learned early on to only say no in serious situations, for immediate safety reasons, such as if Sasha was running into a road. That way, when I did use no, it drew attention from her and would make her stop in her tracks, giving the word more impact than it otherwise would have had for her. We use other phrases to say no. For example, we might say 'maybe later' or 'when you're old enough'. Sometimes we might have to say that we can't afford something. The word 'no' is rarely used, and good explanations are always given for our answers to any requests.

Direct demands should be removed from language wherever possible; we found it helped to rethink lots of the words used to communicate in everyday life. Avoid using need, must or have to in your sentences and instead try the gentler and less threatening options of may, could, would you like, how about, etc. Rephrasing requests in a longer, less demanding way can work wonders: 'I wonder if we might be able to...' or 'I'm not sure how to do this, do you think you can show me?'

Actions can be also phrased as a challenge or fun game rather than a direct demand. So, instead of 'it's time to brush your teeth', we might say 'I bet you can't finish brushing your teeth before I have finished mine' or 'race you to the bathroom'. It is worth bearing in mind that PDA children often need to stay in control though and therefore it is best if they win the game or race. This works with younger children who may not realize that you are trying to come a close second, but we found that after a certain age or awareness level, this did not work so well. Using a third person to enforce rules is a good way of deflecting responsibility for a necessary demand; for example, 'The manager of the ice rink says it needs to close at 4pm, so that is when we need to leave.'

Use humour

We would not have achieved half of what we did with Sasha if we hadn't acted the clown occasionally, or used puns, or turned everyday situations into a slapstick comedy. Phrasing requests light-heartedly can make all the difference. Humour can reduce the intensity of demands and make them feel not so overwhelming. An example might be calling yourself stupid as you pretend not to see the pair of shoes which need putting on right in front of you. Humour can also de-escalate a tense situation, or provide a distraction at difficult times, but use with caution, because once a child is past a certain stage on the approach to meltdown, humour can inflame a situation.

Remain calm

I know it is extremely difficult to use humour and stay calm when you are feeling stressed and all you want to do is leave the house and not be late. PDA children often pick up on your tension though, which in turn adds to their anxiety level, so it is vital to avoid showing your own emotions. No raising your voice or even gritting your teeth because that will be noticed. It might help to decide in advance what your priority is; is it getting wherever you are going on time, in which case you might need to become accustomed to building in extra transition time, or is it simply leaving the house at all? If things are not going to plan, it is unlikely that heightened emotions will work miracles and help to put our children back on track. So, no matter what you are feeling on the inside, don't let it show on the outside.

Reduce demands

Have you ever thought about how many demands are placed on children on an average day? Before even leaving the house, we generally ask them to wake up, get up, brush their teeth, get dressed, eat breakfast, get a bag ready, put their shoes and coat on and more. There are further examples of daily demands which could be added to that list. For a child who is worried about getting any one of those activities wrong, that is a whole heap of extra demands that need to be juggled. Add in any sensory issues, any difficulty with processing information and anxiety about time pressures, all of which tend to be common in autistic individuals, and it is no wonder that a point of overload is reached and a meltdown occurs.

Of course, I am not saying that we can avoid all demands, but we can appreciate the difficulties involved with these cumulative demands and try to make them easier. Are there unidentified sensory issues, are the socks never right, for example? Maybe seamless socks could be considered. Do you need to arrive somewhere by a certain time? Try to allow more time for getting ready, or alternatively consider whether that time for arriving can be pushed back in any way.

It is important to accept that reducing demands at home is not the same as having no boundaries. I always ask myself 'why' if I'm thinking of any rules or demands: what is the point, what do I hope to gain from them and are they likely to work? The boundaries we do have involve understanding right from wrong, and no aggression or being mean. My children do not have to sit at a table to eat with us, they don't have restricted screen time and there are no consequences if they don't brush their teeth every day. Tamsin would cope with these kinds of rules being imposed, but for Sasha, because of her PDA, they would be virtually impossible to stick to. Other families might feel that these demands are absolutely necessary for life to run smoothly in their houses and that is entirely up to them of course. We all have our own opinions, but my feeling is that people should keep their thoughts and judgements to themselves unless they fully understand the situation of any other family. And that is pretty difficult unless they are living with them full time.

Pick your battles (or choose your challenges)

This is not the same as lowering your expectations, although that may also apply in many cases. It is a case of weighing up what matters more to you. Is it clean teeth or is it leaving the house calmly and on time? Obviously, most of us would prefer both of those things to happen, but given that they won't, which do you choose? If you drop the demand for tooth brushing in the morning (not that I'm advocating that, in case my dentist is reading...), are you more likely to be able to leave the house on time that day because the rest of the routine runs smoothly? It might be the choice between your child sitting at the dinner table for a meal, or them eating food with good nutritional value, wherever in the house they choose to eat it. It could be letting them choose to wear no coat in winter because they literally won't leave the house with one on. For every family, the battles will be different, and for every family with a PDA child, the scope of the battles is likely to change frequently (see the point below about being spontaneous).

Tread carefully with routine

Routine can be good, except when you need to be spontaneous. For PDA children and autistic children in general, there can be some comfort in knowing what is expected to happen, as that knowledge reduces anxiety. Conversely, however, being expected to do the same thing every day can be seen as a demand in itself, so some children might want to break free from any routine in order to feel that they are in control. Forward planning and preparation for any event or change in routine was vital for our daughter, and using visual clues and clear instructions at both school and at home definitely helped, but only as long as flexibility was possible.

These are of course only general approaches, and parents often have more specific questions they would like answering, such as 'What do I do when he won't leave the house?' or 'How do I get her to turn the iPad off and go to sleep?' This would need to be an extremely long book to explain all the steps needed to try to find the solution for each specific situation. Every child and every family is different, and any of these approaches may work one day but not the next...

Be cautious with rewards and consequences

The question about whether rewards and consequences work with children who have the PDA profile is one I hear often. Whether I'm asked by teachers struggling to gain control in a classroom, or by parents who have exhausted all the typical parenting strategies, there's always an incredulous look given when I give my response, as if it makes no sense to be given 'no' as the answer. I think whatever the answer is, it relates very closely to what rules, boundaries or beliefs you have as a family. I don't in any way want to challenge how everyone else chooses to live their lives, but I will say that, because of PDA, we have learned to parent in a style which probably falls somewhat outside of 'typical'. A few years after Sasha's diagnosis and the subsequent lightbulb moment, I came across the term gentle parenting. Before having children, I might have dismissed this concept, thinking it was too lenient. Now I can relate to the premise and draw parallels with how we have had to modify our behaviour.

Our experiences have shown us the difference between our older daughter and our PDAer. We parented Tamsin in a traditional, standard kind of way. The same way that we, as her parents, were both brought up. We used typical rewards, consequences and praise. We never needed to do it differently for Tamsin; it just worked. Typical parenting is not easy all the time, I do know that. But I can honestly say, hand on heart, that although there were of course difficult times with our first-born, parenting her through those early years was a million times easier than parenting our PDA child. I think that is only a slight exaggeration.

The reason it is easier is because our eldest girl follows patterns which we ourselves were brought up understanding as children, and which we therefore expected from her. We expected her to do as she was told, after listening to and understanding basic rules. We knew that if she didn't, we could teach her what she was doing wrong by giving her a consequence. Some of the rules which families have at home are often not written down or even expressed at all, and yet children are somehow expected to know and follow them as they grow up. Learning more about autism made me think more about how our older daughter and many other children soak up basic social rules from watching the world around them rather than through direct teaching.

As an example, I can guarantee that I never explicitly told either of our girls not to throw a whole toilet roll down the toilet bowl as they were growing up, and yet our eldest would somehow have known, or deduced, that that was not an action that was going to make her parents happy. Of course, there is a chance that any child, diagnosis or not, might do this at a young age (and teenagers later on who are wanting to cause mischief perhaps), but once they get to a certain age then they seem to realize it is something they should not do. Sasha didn't seem to understand this though. Even when we explained to her after the first time, it didn't stop her from doing it again months later, without any recognition that she was doing wrong. Sasha seemed to have an inability to learn from teaching or from consequences.

Types of consequences used by parents tend to vary between households according to age of the child and depending on what parenting methods have been decided on. One classic example for younger children might be the naughty step; another could be returning a child several times to their bedroom without any attention if they wouldn't settle in an evening. Some methods we used for our eldest may have worked quicker than others, and we may have used different strategies to some other parents, but generally those strategies all came from the rulebook of typical parenting. The type that Supernanny liked to teach. In every situation where we had to use consequences, Tamsin would learn from the experience. She didn't show any distress, and eventually modified her behaviour around that particular issue. Not so for Sasha. It was clear from a young age that even with much repetition, nothing was ever learnt from a consequence. All that happened was that Sasha would display extreme distress if consequences were introduced. As time went on, I began to understand this was a result of the extreme anxiety which is so synonymous with PDA. Natural consequences are what we began to use at home to try to teach this lesson. For example, if a toy or tablet was thrown in anger and broken, and we didn't have the money to replace it, then not having it any more or having to use it with a broken screen would be punishment enough. Because of the way we altered our parenting style due to PDA, I can't remember any instances where Sasha was being wilfully naughty and would deserve a punishment.

So how do we show boundaries if we rarely say no to Sasha? How does she learn right from wrong if we don't use consequences? This is tricky to explain to others who don't live like we do, but I'm pretty sure that those who know us would agree that neither of our daughters is wild and out of control without boundaries. We haven't chosen a free and easy lifestyle, but even if we had, who would have the right to judge? We do have boundaries, but maybe not in the way that traditionalists might recognize them. I think what we find ourselves doing to make sure there are boundaries is talking through many possibilities, differentiating between right and wrong, and always explaining and having good reason for any rules which do exist. Rules are always different from one household to another. We probably have fewer than most. I am sure eyebrows have been raised when I say that Sasha does not sit at a table to eat with us, for example. That is a rule we don't enforce in our house. From a fairly young age, she has been allowed to eat pretty much where she needed to. Sasha knows that other families might usually eat at a table together but that doesn't make it any easier for her. Sensory issues such as smells, tastes and too much sound play a part in her inability to eat with others, but the fact that her brain is always buzzing and she is unable to engage in age-appropriate conversation also plays a big part. We realized that she needs to have her own choice of background sound playing, in a place she is comfortable in, for her to eat happily.

People have sometimes suggested to me that Sasha would be happily eating at a table, as part of a formal sit-down meal now, if we had just forced her to sit at a table when she was younger. And likewise, her diet would be better if we had made her eat a variety of food. Do the people who make those kinds of comments not think that we tried with Sasha? Maybe they don't realize that our older daughter is able to sit at a table with strangers, be polite and follow social norms? We didn't decide to make an effort to teach this kind of societal expectation to Tamsin but not to bother with Sasha. The bottom line is that Sasha's reactions when we tried to make her behave in typical ways when she was younger were extreme, so nothing was achieved by using these parenting methods.

Rewards have rarely worked for Sasha. They have only ever helped if they were immediate, and if the reward to be given was of Sasha's own choosing. The carrot and stick approach has not worked well because the motivational tool needs to be something Sasha really wants, and there seems to be very little she desires enough to make the action worthwhile. Sweets or chocolate, toys or activities, all the usual motivators for children were of little interest to Sasha. Sometimes even the best reward in the world cannot help her get over the block to the perceived demand. Computer games and McDonalds fries have been the only rewards to motivate Sasha that I can bring to mind, but they have only worked at times when Sasha was happy and able to achieve the desired outcome. There can be many outside influences at play which make it difficult for her to achieve, including, but not limited to, sensory difficulties and social interactions. Anxiety is probably the key factor though; anxiety over her ability to perform and anxiety over what will happen next once it is done.

One example of when rewards haven't succeeded in the way they are intended is how Sasha reacted to the school reward system when she started at the MLD school. I didn't think she would show any willingness in the idea that if she did well at her work, or what the teacher asked her to do, then she would be allowed to choose a reward from a set offering, but I was willing to let them try of course. The rewards included items such as a selection of toys or games that were on display in a cabinet, or the choice of a monetary high street voucher, or the option to exchange rewards for non-school uniform days. There hadn't been any rewards like this on offer at her mainstream school, and for the first few weeks of the new school, commonly known as the honeymoon period, Sasha seemed to go along with the novelty factor of this system. She soon started building up rewards by completing easy worksheets, and her reward of choice was going to be some non-school uniform days. As the demands increased though, the novelty wore off. Sasha quickly gained enough points so she could have a whole week of non-uniform, but she then struggled with anxiety over the fact that she would be going to school looking different from all the other children. So, she didn't do it and instead she stressed about not cashing in on the reward. She had no interest in any of the other rewards though, and the teacher then found it impossible to get Sasha to produce work in return for a reward.

A sticker chart or promise of a reward may work for some children in the short term, but then again, it may not. I totally understand when others are confused and ask, 'But if she's done that once, why won't she do it again?' The not-so-simple answer to that is that PDA children are spending a huge amount of time trying to cope with different pressures, some of which you can see and some which are not so obvious to those of us who do not have the same internal struggles. Praise is another area of life that seems to cause our PDAer problems. She doesn't react well to being told she has done well and I am not allowed to ask for a high five or show any other signs of happiness at her achievements. One theory is that praise is a demand in itself – an expectation that the stakes will be raised and greater levels need to be achieved the next time. For someone who struggles with anxiety and expectation, it is easy to see why this might be an issue. It is impossible to say that praise, rewards and consequences do not work at all for PDA children though. Nothing to do with PDA is ever that simple.

Changing your lenses is so important. When you accept that your child is not refusing or avoiding or having a meltdown just to be oppositional or awkward, but rather because of an underlying extremely high level of anxiety, then you can start to find solutions. Letting go of some of the traditional parenting techniques that simply don't work may just lead to a calmer life all round. I wish I could personally help every family that faces daily challenges at home. We have experienced plenty of those difficult times and I understand how physically and mentally exhausting they can be. I also wish I could give everyone an assurance that what works for us will work for them, but every child is different and every family faces different situations in life. What we have learnt over the years is that all of the ways we try to help our child may work for a few days or weeks, then may not seem to work over the next few weeks, but will possibly work again when tried in months or years to come. Or they might never work again, ever. That doesn't mean we stop trying. As parents we have had to learn to be prepared, to adapt to different situations at different ages, to be flexible and to let go of our own expectations.

WAYS TO HELP CHILDREN WITH PATHOLOGICAL DEMAND AVOIDANCE

- Plan ahead

- Be flexible

- Build a trusting relationship

- Offer choices

- Choose words carefully

- Use humour

- Remain calm

- Reduce demands

- Pick your battles (or choose your challenges)

- Tread carefully with routine

- Be cautious with rewards and consequences.

EPILoGUE: THE FUTURE

Sasha received a diagnosis of autism over 13 years ago, at the age of two. The fact that it was so long ago, and she was so young at the time, has meant that she remembers very little of the appointments and observations that were made. Although she was present for the assessments, it wasn't possible to involve her in those initial discussions. Lots of parents ask when the right time is to tell your child they are autistic, and how you should tell them. We waited until Sasha showed some awareness of being different, then we tried to slowly pass on small snippets of information rather than sit her down for a long serious talk about it. At the age of nine she was struggling to explain her more frequent upsets, and told me that she couldn't find the right words to tell me what was going on for her. I asked if she had noticed that she found things a bit more difficult than some of the other children in her class. She thought about it for a minute or two, then suggested that maybe she felt more stressed more of the time than the other children did. When she became a teenager, she began to question her diagnosis of autism. I think she has struggled to understand what autism means. Even for adults with more life experience, there is much to learn and understand about autism. Helping Sasha to understand more about it is difficult because she is not open to conversation – even when she asks questions, she is rarely happy to listen to anything other than a very short answer. She has asked us on occasion, 'But what does autism mean for me? How does it affect me?' I have to hope that the short answers I have been able to give will spark a desire in her to explore the topic more in her own way in the future, if that is what she wants of course.

As parents, we have no doubt that the diagnosis of autism was right for her, and I am as certain now as I was when I first read the characteristics of Pathological Demand Avoidance that her profile is that of PDA. That doesn't mean we are disregarding Sasha's thoughts; we do understand why she might struggle with her own identity. We have discussed with Sasha the possibility of returning to a clinician for a new assessment so that she might be more engaged in the process this time, but that brings with it lots of challenges. Having to respond to questioning is not something Sasha can do easily and she would need to feel comfortable and ready to go through that process. The cost of these assessments is also a factor because Sasha worries a lot about what we are spending our money on and doesn't want us to pay out for more assessments. I will admit to some parental guilt about this because when Sasha was younger I would regularly tell her that we didn't have lots of money spare to spend on computer games. This was one way that I tried to distract and redirect Sasha, to avoid us going bankrupt! This has possibly led to Sasha worrying about finances more than necessary (although better for it to be this way around, I feel!).

If we were to repeat the assessment process, I would ask for ADHD (Attention Deficit Hyperactivity Disorder) to be considered this time. When Sasha was around six years old it was mentioned as a possibility and both we and school were given a Conners questionnaire to complete. Our responses indicated that Sasha might qualify for an ADHD diagnosis but the responses from school suggested she didn't quite meet the threshold. On reflection, I wonder if that was because whoever completed the form was more used to seeing a hyperactive presentation of ADHD. Sasha wasn't outwardly hyperactive; she wasn't the kind of child who was bouncing around all over the place. However, the feedback we always got about her attention levels was that she found it difficult to concentrate. I have researched the subject of ADHD in the past few years and can see Sasha's symptoms of inattention, distractibility and poor working memory. From what I have heard, a large proportion of autistic people (but by no means all) are also diagnosed with ADHD.

When she was younger there didn't seem much point in pressing for a diagnosis of ADHD for Sasha, given that she always refused to take any medicine (and still does). Medication is a wide subject and here is not the place for any detail on this, but it is covered in many other books. We have heard that it can give some individuals diagnosed with ADHD an improvement in their focus and this could be a consideration for Sasha in later life. Other methods to help manage ADHD tend to involve lifestyle changes (better diet, better sleep habits and more exercise, for example), but Sasha's PDA means that even if she did agree these changes might help, her avoidance of the demands could make implementing them difficult. Likewise with anxiety; there are medications proven to help in some cases but I suspect they might not have much impact on the high and overwhelming anxiety levels that PDAers live with every day. I know there is much talk online about the crossovers between ADHD and PDA, but I also know that a diagnosis of autism with ADHD would not describe our daughter fully in the way that PDA does.

I cannot stress enough that having the right people and attitudes involved when it comes to helping PDA individuals is so important. There have only been a handful of people over the years who have been able to really connect and chat with Sasha about how she feels. They have managed both because of their understanding of autism, and PDA more specifically, but also because of their great attitudes, fun and flexible approaches. When people like this come into the life of a parent of a PDA child, I don't know if they realize just how much of a difference they make. I have been grateful to them because there are so few who have been able to foster a trust relationship that enables Sasha to feel heard. Some only spent a relatively short amount of time with Sasha, but their understanding and compassion enabled her to feel comfortable with them.

The discussion around whether PDA is real or not may never end. I respect other opinions, but trying to highlight the existence of PDA has been a focus of my life over the last 12 years because I believe more understanding will help my daughter. I am not sure the term PDA on its own achieves that though, which is why I have felt it necessary to share personal examples of how certain situations have made her feel and react over the years.

As a parent, my greatest worry for Sasha's future is that she might develop mental health issues because of the difficulties she has had with accessing school and maintaining friendships. These have led to low self-esteem for Sasha and it is not easy to think of ways to build her back up. Recently, there has been much talk of the mental health crisis surrounding children. Being a teenager is hard enough anyway and I actually feel that one of the upsides of Sasha no longer being in school is that she is not constantly comparing herself to others. There have been times over the past few years when Sasha's mood has dipped worryingly; one time she found her old school yearbook at home and became very nostalgic about her classmates from the mainstream school. For a while after that she was almost inconsolable, not happy with anything or anyone, least of all herself. It hurts to hear your child say, 'What's the point in anything? What's the point in me? I don't want to do anything; everything is too difficult.' For the Tribunal we had to attend, Sasha submitted her typed thoughts about what had happened for her in terms of school, and they were very insightful. One line she wrote has stuck in my mind:

'I was just tired. Tired of this endless cycle of trying, hoping, failing, feeling, repeating.' She calls herself all sorts of names that I'd rather she didn't – weird, sucky, nerdy, outcast, and more.

During one bedtime chat in recent years, Sasha told me that she worried for the world because she was sure the ratio would eventually go up to 100 per cent of people being autistic. I tried to counter these thoughts with examples of autistic people who have achieved good things and then I asked why she thought all the population being autistic would be bad. Her reply was that it would be worse because of all the worries, because autistic people have lots of worries.

I chatted with Sasha to see if I could include more of her views in this book, with her agreement. My interview questions were not up to much though and she told me that in no uncertain terms! I will share some of the questions and responses, but I think it is clear to see what I mean when I say Sasha does not like questions. I had probably already overstayed my welcome in her room after just the first one...

Me: How does it make you feel if you are asked or told to do something?

Sasha: Depends what I'm asked to do. You need to be more specific.

Me: How do you feel if someone tries to make you do something right now and not in your own time?

Sasha: It doesn't make me feel. I don't know how I feel.

Me: What was good about school?

Sasha: Potatoes and jelly.

Me: What was not good about school?

Sasha: Everything else.

Me: How would you describe yourself?

Sasha: I wouldn't.

Me: What are you interested in?

Sasha: A lot. A wide variety, too broad and too specific at the same time. The peak of my interests rotates every two weeks or so on average.

Me: Do you remember having meltdowns when you were younger?

Sasha: I can remember countless times when I curled up in the corner. I was angry but I didn't want to get into trouble. I don't want other people to get angry at me and I'm scared of repercussions.

Me: What would you like to do in the future?

Sasha: Drawing and making animations.

I would have loved for everyone to read all of her thoughts on life. I hope that at some point in the future she might be ready to tell her story in some way. The chances are that if her storytelling was to happen, she would be more likely to do that through an animated video or a series of digital art rather than any kind of writing. She is still not a fan of books and there are only a handful that have grabbed her attention over the years. We've tried suggesting different formats – comics or graphic novels, kindle or audiobooks – but nothing has been welcomed. We would love her to enjoy books in any format but, as with everything else, that would only happen on her terms, if and when she is ready to make that change. This does not mean, however, that she is not knowledgeable. Sasha has soaked up so much information via the Internet; YouTube can be such a great learning tool. She has also typed many amazing fan-fiction stories on her iPad, something that I know would not have happened if she had only had access to pen and paper.

Words I use to describe Sasha are funny, perceptive, quick-witted, intelligent, caring, sociable, imaginative, creative, passionate, determined and loving. She has many strengths and good attributes and I hope more people will get to see them over the years to come. I think it is important for everyone to keep the positives of their child in mind, because it can be totally exhausting parenting a PDA child. It helps to remind ourselves that our children are amazing, and that they are not being oppositional to annoy us!

Our main wish for Sasha, the same as it is for our older daughter, is happiness. Independence is also on that wish list, but we don't know at what stage that will come. Like most parents, we would like to see her living her own life happily, with us providing light, rather than full, support. Sasha is 15 now; who can tell what the future will bring for any child? Never say never is one of my favourite phrases. I will never stop encouraging and supporting her to achieve whatever she wants to do.